In *MissioRelate*, we finally have a book on small grou[...] Scott understands small groups is about Christian disc[...] apart from mission. In order to get here, however, we [...] lying changes necessary to lead the church into mission via small groups. In *MissioRelate* Scott Boren gives us such a way. He proves himself that rare practitioner who knows both theology and culture sufficient enough to guide us well.

—*David Fitch, BR Lindner Chair of Evangelical Theology, Northern Seminary and Author of* The End of Evangelicalism?

In the missional context that now lies before us, existing styles of small groups based on affinity where people are shaped by an assumed 'church-language' are increasingly irrelevant and archaic. Scott has been wrestling with the question of how to form groups that engage with our new missional context. He shows us how to enter our stories and form groups that make a difference.

— *Alan Roxburgh, President, The Missional Network and author of* Missional

When I read *Missional Small Groups*, Scott Boren reminded me that small groups done well can produce revolutionary change in the lives of individuals, in communities, and even across the world. Now, after reading *MissioRelate,* Scott has convinced me that such groups can develop and thrive in any church . . . even my own.

— *Sam O'Neal, Managing Editor, smallgroups.com*

MissioRelate is a thoughtful treatment of the place where small groups intersect with missional ministry. Boren takes small groups out of the peripheral role they play in most churches and moves them into the grassroots organizing principle for ministry. If you're ready to create new church leadership rhythms, *MissioRelate* will be extremely helpful in your search.

— *Dr. Bob Logan, founder of Logan Leadership and Journey Together Now*

I am convinced that every small groups pastor should read *MissioRelate*. Scott has unearthed what may be the new guide for doing groups in this era. Many books challenge our perspective of doing groups. This one will change your perspective, demand a new way of thinking, and set you free to let God do what only God can do through your groups.

— *Rick Howerton, Global Small Group Environmentalist for NavPress, and author of* Destination Community

Small group ministry continues to be a crucial dimension of vibrant church life. In *MissioRelate*, Scott Boren provides the reader with deep insight into why this is the case while offering substantive guidance for the development of small group ministry. He especially makes the critical connection between congregation and context that this ministry provides when approached from a missional perspective. This book is a must-read for anyone who takes seriously the importance of cultivating small groups as a primary aspect of congregational ministry.

— *Craig Van Gelder, Ph.D., Professor of Congregational Mission, Luther Seminary*

If you are ready for a powerful mental and spiritual adjustment regarding small groups, *MissioRelate* is for you! This book should be read by anyone wanting to reach their culture for Christ while making growing disciples.

— *Alan Danielson, Author and Pastor of New Life Bible Church, in Norman, OK*

If you're looking for a way to move your small group ministry from "connecting in community" to "impacting communities," *MissioRelate* is a must read. If you're like me, you will be challenged by Part 2. Trust me . . . it's worth a very careful read. With that foundation, Part 3 will get a lot of use as all of us move in the missional direction.

— *Mark Howell, Community Life Pastor, Parkview Christian Church, Consultant, and owner of smallgroupresources.net*

If you want to move beyond the next missional formula for small groups and equip people to cultivate a way of life where they join with others and God to make a difference in the world, then you need to read this book. In *MissioRelate*, Scott Boren asks questions which have the power to move the church from shallow definitions of success to deep missional engagement in the world for the sake of the world. This book is a gift to the church, for it will help us live lives that are faithful to the God of Mission.

— *JR Woodward, Co-founder of Kairos LA and the Ecclesia Network, Activist, Blogger (jrwoodward.net) and Author of* ViralHope

I own more than a hundred books on small groups, and I am not overstating my case when I say this book is different than all of them! *MissioRelate* is a game changer and a page turner. It will challenge your normal small group paradigm while encouraging you with what God can do in your church by living in the natural rhythms of a missional way of life.

— *Michael Mack, Small Groups Pastor, Northeast Christian Church, Louisville, KY, and author of* Small Group Vital Signs.

The word "missional" seems to be abuzz across the landscape of the American church. It's "hip" to be missional! What I love about *MissioRelate* is that Scott plainly lays out the foundations of what it takes for small groups to be truly missional, both theologically and practically. This book will change the way you think about small groups . . . In a good way!

— *Ben Reed, Director of Community Groups, Grace Community Church, Clarksville, TN.*

Scott's four "stories" drove the nail all the way into the board for me. These are anointed insights by a man who has been gifted with both wisdom and the skill to write clearly. I was greatly impacted Scott's presentation in MissioRelate. This is going to become a classic in the field of small group literature. Join me in thanking the Lord for his stewardship and contribution to the Kingdom.

— *Dr. Ralph W. Neighbour, Jr., Founder, TOUCH Outreach Ministries and author of* Christ's Basic Bodies

missiorelate

missiorelate

m. scott boren

becoming a church of
missional small groups

TOUCH Publications, Inc
Houston, Texas

Published by TOUCH Publications
P.O. Box 7847, Houston, Texas 77270 USA
800-735-5865 • www.touchusa.org

Printed in the United States of America

Cover design: www.neubauerdesign.com
Editor: Randall G. Neighbour

International Standard Book Number: 978-0-9825352-4-0

TOUCH Publications is the book-publishing division of
TOUCH Outreach Ministries, a resource and consulting ministry
for churches with a vision for missional small groups.

Connect with the author through his web site:
www.mscottboren.com

acknowledgements/dedication

When I first started writing, a friend told me, "Writers write." Those words have stuck with me as I cannot seem to *not* write. Writing is something that eats up a lot of alone time, but it is never done in isolation. Penned words might come through an individual, but no book is written on an island. Ideas arise in community and this is definitely the case here. Mentors like Alan Roxburgh, Gordon Fee, Jim Egli, Ralph Neighbour, Bill Beckham, and James Bell have shaped my thinking and ministry. Friends like Randall Neighbour, Joel Comiskey, Greg Boyd, Paul Eddy, Janice Rohling, Kevin Callaghan, and many others have shared parts of my ministry journey and have shaped my life and thinking. Thinkers both historical and contemporary like Deitrich Bonhoeffer, Lesslie Newbigin, N. T. Wright, Colin Greene, Martin Robinson, Craig Van Gelder, David Fitch and Stanley Hauerwas have served as towers of input. Such people stand behind my words, and to them I owe the best parts. I'll claim all of the weaknesses as my own. I could go on and on, but the time keeper is telling me that the time is up.

My beautiful bride, Shawna shapes my immediate earthly community, along with our four kids. To them I dedicate these words, hoping that they contribute to the shaping of new ways of being God's people in the days to come.

contents

preface

I enjoy reading the back-story of how a book is developed, so I thought I would try my hand at it. Let me first state that this book is an accident, at least as much as it is possible for something that takes so much work to be called an accident. I never intended to write it. In fact, after completing my last book, I told a friend I did not want to write another book on groups for a while. So how did this accident happen?

First, there were three chapters that I could not include in *Missional Small Groups* because the intended audience was group leaders. These three chapters were written for church leaders and pastors. While consulting with pastors on the phone, I would send them these chapters and their feedback revealed that the information was helpful.

So I called up my friend Randall Neighbour and asked him if his ministry would publish a revision of my earlier book *The Relational Way* by inserting these new chapters. He liked the idea, so I prepared the chapters and sent them to him. Oddly enough, the layout file was corrupt and could not be recovered. The only solution was to scan or rekey the original text.

At this point, I suggested a completely new book. My idea was to put these three chapters with some other material I had written or taught through the last couple of years. I remember telling Randall I thought I had enough to create a 100-page booklet. To my surprise, I found more than 100 pages. Far more!

Believe it or not, this book came together over a period of weeks. As soon as Randall and I agreed on a new title, something snapped inside my mind and I churned out words faster than Carl Lewis running on a six pack of Red Bull. For this reason, this may very well be my best book yet. I find that when words flow quickly, I speak from my heart. Conversely, it might be my worst book to date. I have put myself "out there" in this book by speaking from my experience and without providing lots of supporting evidence, footnotes, quotes, or statistics. It's raw, and it lacks nuance. Some readers will love this. Others will read the book and wish I'd been more balanced. With all this in mind, please indulge me. I'm a brash Texan living in Minnesota where nice is very important. *Missional Small Groups* is my *nice* book. This one is less so, even though I still attempt to keep the feather ruffling to a minimum. The reality is that what I'm writing about in this book has changed everything for me.

One final thought: After completing the manuscript, I realized that this resource works hand-in-glove with *The Relational Way*. The ten chapters in that book provide a theological nuance and justification to the ten chapters in part two of this book, helping a leadership team of a church lead their groups into MissioRelate. And taking it one step further, these resources, coupled with the resources for group leaders (*Missional Small Groups* and the companion study guide), provide a foundation for something that has changed almost everything I have thought about small groups.

— M. Scott Boren

By the way, I'd love to know what you think about the content and where it takes you and your church via Twitter: @mscottboren or on my website: www.mscottboren.com. I look forward to learning your thoughts and entering into a deeper dialog.

I literally grew up in the church. We lived less than a mile from the building where we worshipped. My dad was a deacon and my mom was the only member who played the piano. She was also the church treasurer. My paternal grandfather and maternal grandmother as well as my aunt Pat and Uncle Wimpy — yes that was his name — were faithful members. Three church services a week plus Sunday school and quite a few other activities filled my days and nights. When combined with annual week long revival meetings, summer church camp, Christian concerts, and retreats, the traditional church formed the rhythms of my life.

Just before my senior year of high school, I felt God's leading to devote my life to full-time church leadership. After my first sermon, an 80-year old deacon told me, "I just heard the best sermon of my life!" (I think he just liked me.) I then went off to college and quickly found my way into leadership of a youth group. During the summer months, I worked as an intern in a church's youth ministry and then went to Germany to be a summer youth minister.

Because of the environment in which I was raised, I knew how church worked. It was a part of my life story. I knew its language, its patterns, and what I call its rhythms. I also knew how to make church work, but not because I had read books about church leadership or attended seminars on how to run a church. I knew how to do church naturally because its rhythms were a part of me.

During my last year of undergraduate studies, I made plans to go to seminary. I wanted to be a preacher, following in the footsteps of role models like Chuck Swindoll, Joel Gregory, and Louie Giglio. My well-laid plans were abruptly interrupted when I investigated how the early church was organized to form people into organic community and how God was moving through churches throughout the world through small groups. After just a few months of exploration, I clearly saw that the way we use the pulpit in the modern church actually requires an overemphasis of the skills and charisma of uniquely gifted people. Plenty of my friends felt called to that kind of ministry. I, on the other hand, found a different calling: helping others form patterns of church life that facilitated organic or "bottom-up" life through small groups.

When I first wrestled with this shift in calling, I was taking a senior level class on leading organizational change. For one of the assignments, I interviewed someone who had grown up in an experimental church while his pastor/father tried to figure out what organic or missional small groups might look like in the 1970s. After he answered my questions, I told him of my plans to go to seminary. His response was not what I expected. He said, "Why would you do that if God is calling you to do this?"

I ignored his challenge and went to seminary as planned, which lasted all of one semester. Within a few weeks of classes and interaction with professors, I realized I was being trained to lead the kind of church that most people who had little or no church background cared about! During those seminary months, I was asking different questions and no one there had the answers I needed. I found others who had these same questions about the church. The labels for what they talked about came in many different forms: a small group church; a cell church; a church of small groups; meta church; and Groups of 12 (just to name a few of many). Before I knew any of these terms or titles, I simply caught a vision for missional life lived out through relational connections in small groups. While grateful for the church that I knew so well, I saw a fresh way of being the church that seemed to hold greater promise. Knowing this created a challenge: *I had a new vision, but the old church rhythms dominated my imagination. I had to learn to play new music that fit this new vision.*

finding new leadership rhythms

The search for new rhythms generated two important paths. The first was the school of hard knocks. I was immersed in small group life when I left seminary and joined an experimental church in Houston. This led to roles of small group leadership, pastoring small groups in two different cities, and eventually overseeing a team of small group pastors in still another city.

The second path has come through my unquenchable curiosity. I love to research and I've learned a great deal about new leadership rhythms through my work for a small group training and consulting organization. For a number of years, I worked with churches in this venture before it became a popular trend in the West. I started out by answering phones and addressing basic questions posed by pastors. This developed into a role where I helped small group authors develop their message, which led me to a three-year research project and my first book. For the last 18 years, I have immersed myself in the world of small groups to find the rhythms of leadership that develop small groups that are missional, relational, and transformational. As I look back on this journey, I find that it parallels the trends that have shaped the imaginations of pastors and leaders over the last 20 years. To illustrate this clearly, let me break down this journey into five stages.

Stage one: The call to something radical
From the 1950s through the late 1980s, talk about small groups was characterized by a radical and costly call to Christian community that appealed to a minority of church leaders and their churches. The focus did not lie so much on growth and numbers, but the quality of life that stood in stark contrast to traditional ways of being the church. This can be seen in the rather

controversial writings of Ralph W. Neighbour, Jr.; Thom Wolf, the former pastor of the church now called Mosiac; the training that came out of The Church of the Savior in Washington D.C.; and the more theological work of Elton Trueblood and Howard Snyder.

Stage two: The focus on structures

In the early 1990s, there was a subtle shift from the radical call of a life lived in community to a strong emphasis on church structures. This time was characterized by a heavy confrontation of traditional church forms and a clear articulation of new, small-group-centered church structures. While the first stage was focused on the life or the "wine" that a church might experience, this second stage was focused on the "wineskins" and an urgent need for new ones. In some circles, the old wineskins were castigated and even labeled as demonic while the new wineskin that was being presented was a revelation for the church. As one might imagine, this stage weeded out a number of potentially interested pastors and churches due to its dogmatic tone.

Stage three: The popularization of small groups

By 1995, small groups and small group principles were promoted by more mainstream church leaders and consultants. Carl George, Peter Wagner, Thom Rainer, and others highlighted the importance of small groups to bring balance to church life. This emphasis—coming from these respected voices—created a paradigm shift. Small groups changed from being something radical (embraced only by innovators) to something that middle-of-the-road churches could successfully embrace. In other words, small groups became a credible church growth mechanism. By the end of the decade, Willow Creek Community Church trumpeted the importance of small groups publicly and two of their staff pastors released a book entitled, *Building a Church of Small Groups*. This stage brought a fresh new wave of small groups that washed across the American church.

The emphasis on structures in stages two and three did not address my need for a new set of rhythms for leading the church, so I formed a completely new set of questions in my quest. After all, one could set up the right organization and develop all of the right materials to support it, but still miss the development of the rhythms so fundamental to missional group life. Structures alone were not enough for me. In fact, I discovered that there are a lot of growing, sound church structures, but the life produced within their small groups was far from the vision God gave me of missional life lived out relationally. These churches are simply "enfolding" people into groups who continue to live like most other people in our western culture.

Stage four: A focus on understanding change

The small group organization I worked for in the 1990s focused on helping churches make a transition from traditional church life to missional community lived out through small groups. To be frank, our failure rate was alarming. Pastors and core leaders of churches with whom we were working *hoped* their groups of members would take off and reach the lost, but the reality was that most barely got off the ground. They clearly understood how to implement the structures and strategies. What they did not understand was how to lead their people into these new supportive structures and strategies with radical changes in lifestyle.

Through an intensive three-year research project, I analyzed over 50 churches to determine the differences between how successful churches transitioned compared to those who failed. The research gave me enough solid information to develop an 8-stage transition process, resulting in a book called *How Do We Get There From Here?* In this book, I propose a change process for changing a traditional church structure to a small group based church structure, with the goal of developing missional life in those small groups.

By the time this resource was published, there were quite a few books and training seminars on leading change in the church. While most of it was sound information and went deeper than the focus on structures found in stages 2 and 3, ultimately the focus lay on changing structures, not personal and community transformation.

Stage five: A look at how we live

To move beyond nominal group life and small group ministry, I looked beyond new structures. The work of Randy Frazee influenced me as much as anyone at the time. While pastoring in the Dallas/Fort Worth area, he found that the way people operate in normal life directly impacts the way a church experiences missional community. He brought to light that working a sixty-hour work week, commuting an hour or more each day, and enrolling one's children in multiple extra-curricular activities cannot be ignored when developing a strategy to implement or expand a church's small groups. The church, like our own bodies, needs a skeletal system or a structure for support. However, if we *only* have a skeletal system, our bodies do not have life. The other systems are required to bring the bones to life. When these others systems are in place, small group structures of many different kinds can actually produce dynamic missional life that is highly relational.[1]

the parallel stage of normalization

Running alongside these five stages I found yet another pattern of doing small groups I call *normalization*. All along, there have been those who embraced the small group strategy simply for helping people do church just a little better. Groups were formed to close the back door, enfold people into formal membership, and provide off-campus Bible study and/or fellowship in homes between weekend services.

Normalization is not new for the church. It has been performed for decades through various means. Groups have been used to support average Christians living average lives that fit squarely into the average culture outside the four walls of the church building. While I don't think this is necessarily evil, it does create confusion. In this parallel stage, the goal of small group involvement is significantly different than the original vision. Instead of groups being a crucible for community, discipleship, life transformation, and evangelism, normalized small groups in America are nothing more than nice little groups of traditional Christians who gather because it's fun to hang out with other traditional Christians.

What saddens me is not the existence of normalized small groups: I celebrate such groups because they help people take baby steps toward and move some people into new realities with Christ. I am, however, deeply saddened by those who normalize this watered-down experience and promote it as the main goal of group life. Simple involvement or group attendance is the key and the focus in normalization and 80% or 100% participation in groups is the mark of celebration. Instead of pastors generating a completely new way of life through groups, the focus lies on simply connecting people to groups. By confession, I've heard pastors of some of the most "successful" small group systems freely admit that they have no idea what really goes on in their groups. Over the last ten years, there have been many different books that have promoted this experience, some penned by these very pastors.

where are we now?

In some ways, I feel like we are at a crossroads when it comes to the experience of community through small groups. We have choices to make as church leaders:

Option #1: Programmatic

We can choose to continue to focus on structures and look for the latest program to be promoted, one that promises a new small group panacea. These programs might come in the form of new curriculum, a church-wide campaign, or semester groups. The options are abundant. This option will be offered for a long time to come because—for some odd reason—we continue to fall for their hollow promises! Now don't get me wrong. I want to learn from others and I use many of these programs to help pastor my people. But I cannot be satisfied with a programmatic way of doing groups. Such will only produce more of the same and I want something completely different.

Option #2: Organic church

Over the last few years, the organic church has become quite popular. Usually this organic route resembles some of what was experienced by many in Stage 1. There is a call to radical community coupled with a castigation of traditional church life. The form of organic churches usually takes that of a house church, some of which are totally independent while others are regionally connected. There are many writers who have developed some very helpful resources for this option. However, contrary to their belief that the traditional church must be cast aside like a dirty, torn shirt, this is not the *only, most likely*, nor the *primary* option God has for the future of the church.

I've been down the road of trashing the traditional church to elevate my current and "correct" biblical vision for what the church should be. In the end, it only served to produce the same kind of unsatisfactory life in our small groups that we experienced in the traditional church. Birthing a house church that is free of programs and buildings does not automatically result in a transformational body of Christ that is on mission in this world. I am committed to experiencing organic, missional life together, but the either/or foundational attitude on which this option is built gives me pause. I have become very leery of those who claim that they have found the secret insight into the future of the church. I'm sure that they have found one of the ways that God will manifest his life through his people, but we need much more than new structures.[2]

Option #3: Missional small groups

Of course, I'm going to present what I believe to be the best option at this point. If I did not believe this, I would not be writing this book. Last year I wrote a book entitled *Missional Small Groups*. There I wrote to group leaders and group members about small group rhythms that results in world-changing missional community. I seek to move beyond the categories of either/or, either programmatic groups or organic groups. I introduced the idea of missional life being a rhythm that we learn to play as a group. The crux of the book was: if we are going to play such rhythms, we must embrace both good structures and seek to live out the organic life together in community.

Let me state this up front: When I write "Missional Small Groups," I am not referring to a specific number of people or a gathering place. In the chapters to come, I emphasize a way of life and the form that missional life can take in a community in various forms. In some contexts, small groups of 8-15 can be quite missional. In others, small groups might network with three to five other small groups to practice missional life. In yet other situations, the context might call for a missional community of 20-50 people where sub-groups form from within.

please indulge my repetition

I want to be clear: I am not prescribing a specific form called *MissioRelate*. Anyone that says that they have found a missional form gives me cause for caution. I am far more interested in discovering a way of life together by encouraging the leaders within a specific situation to follow the guidance of the Holy Spirit to discover and embrace the most productive missional form.

Now don't come to the conclusion that I feel we should toss out structures or traditions and go totally organic. As soon as we discard our heritage, we lose our bearings. I once thought that we should take this option, but after seeing how God has been at work in the church for the last 2000 years—even with all the weaknesses of the traditional church—I can no longer move in that direction. At the same time, the way ahead for the experience of missional life cannot be orchestrated through a program. When we do this we assume that we can give easy answers to difficult questions. It's more than finding a programmatic system or structure that enfolds 80%, 100%, or even 120% of our weekend attendance into groups. It's more than simply being geographic or developing neighborhood groups. It's so much more than instituting some kind of house church structure that is bigger than a small group but smaller than a small church. And it's far more than aiming to go organic and trying to get back to some kind predetermined idea of what the church did in the New Testament. Church leaders want a plan or a pattern to copy, but I cannot in good conscience point people in this direction. It just doesn't consistently produce missional groups.

This book will point you toward the church leadership rhythms that create a church-wide environment where groups can learn to play the music found in missional small groups. I call this MissioRelate. The pages that follow seek to answer the question: What are the shifts in mindsets and practices required of pastors, leaders, small group champions, and overseers of groups in order to develop groups that live out MissioRelate? (The shorthand question would be: How do we become a church of missional groups?)

Join me and let's see what kind of music we can create.

a vision that
changes everything

missiorelate
*An experience with others and God
that makes a difference in the world*

"normal" groups or missiorelate?

I love books. I must confess that I like to read, research, learn from, and accumulate books. My wife does not completely understand my unusual passion for them, even though she has a similar pension for other products, of which I won't mention. Frankly, I am not sure I understand my love of books either, but it has been a life-long affair. As a child, I recall my father taking me to a used bookstore and selecting just one book. He told me I could have more, but I said one was enough. That night, I remember crying myself to sleep because I did not take him up on his offer.

When you combine my passion for books and the fact that I have been working in the small group arena for almost 20 years, I have more than my fair share of dead trees pressed into white sheets and covered with lots of black ink lining my shelves. As I survey my collection of small group resources, it's obvious that the number of books published on the topic has skyrocketed over the last decade. In the mid-1990s, an author could write something on small groups and church leaders would jump on it as if it was a rare diamond. Today, if you search Amazon.com for " small groups" you will discover nearly six thousand choices of books to read on the topic.

Some of these books are written by well-known pastors and make audacious claims. They pronounce that by adopting their strategy, you will realize a small group "miracle moment" that will suddenly cause your groups to soar with success. These authors act as if they have found a "magic bullet" that none of the other small group thinkers or writers have thought about over the last 50 years. One promises that their strategy will get 100% of your Sunday attendees into groups. Another pastor claims 120% can be procured. The promotional material of yet a third book states, "The greatest challenge facing most churches today isn't getting people through the front door—it's keeping them from leaving through the back door." When I read this, I wanted to scream, "Really? What about the 80% of American churches that are under 100 people?" For the most part, these small churches are comprised of faithful people led by faithful pastors, but they are not seeing droves of first-time visitors each week.

To say the least, all these books with all their claims left me frustrated. So I picked up some old, out-of-print books written by those I call "small-group prophets" from the 1950s-1970s. These include: *Call to Commitment* by Elizabeth O'Connor; *The Seven Last Words of the Church* by Ralph W. Neighbour, Jr.; *Company of the Committed* by Elton Trueblood; and the writings like those of Thom Wolf (the predecessor and former mentor of Erwin McManus at Church on Brady in L.A., now called Mosaic). These voices speak of prophetic test cases or creative experiments that are roots of what we see in small groups today.

When I compared these prophetic books to the new and frustrating books I've read of late, I realized that the fundamental imaginations behind them were quite different. The new voices pointed to structures and small group programs that churches could adopt quite easily, but the lived-out experience of the groups that these books described was quite "normal." What I mean by this is that the groups were designed in such a way to fit quite nicely into the flow of normal life in America. But the imagination of those prophets was shaped by a vision that was anything but normal. While they did not use the word *missional*, they talked of groups of people that were making a difference in the world. It was radical for its time and truthfully, it is still radical for today's church.

Too often, we settle for *normal* groups and we don't even realize it. *Normal* has become so much a part of who we are that when we develop a good program that produces normal groups, we think we have something to brag about. We fail to see that there is more. Far more. This more is *so much more* than something called "small groups" or even "missional small groups." It is a life experienced together that I call MissioRelate.

MissioRelate
An experience with others and God
that makes a difference in the world.

---

stepping back to see God's bigger picture

The development of small groups and their broadly accepted popularity today is something for which our forerunners have fought hard and long. These pioneers sacrificed security, reputation, and success to experience it first-hand. They experimented in a day when they knew that they would experience more failure than success, yet they were compelled to learn a new way of being God's people. Today we stand on their shoulders and we are part of something much larger than the creative ideas we implement. God has been at work in the church for a long time, and he continues to do his work in shaping a bride that will be prepared for his return.

However, in our need to accomplish goals, maintain busy schedules, and survive as pastors, we get caught up in the now. We have failed to see that we are a part of a larger historical move of God that has both a rich history and a powerful future. In our short-sightedness, we want everyone in groups and we want it *now*. We run to those who promise quick results, usually pitched or delivered as "small groups in a box." It's purchased, unwrapped, and then in a great hurry we implement some other church's program. When it does not produce results, we search for and buy into the next program to come along and the insanity deepens.

What we need is a strong dose of God-shaped perspective. Our short-term thinking blinds us to see God's vision for the kingdom, a movement that cannot be created by adopting the latest and greatest ideas developed in

California, Texas, or New York. God is shaping a movement of people relating together on mission, which will not be promoted by a mega church or charismatic personality hawking one big programmatic push for missional living through small groups.

In the book, *Good to Great*, Jim Collins writes about companies that stand out and what they do that is different than those who are average. He and his team of researchers discovered that great companies practice patterns that result in the "flywheel effect." Imagine a huge flywheel, one three stories high and weighing over 5000 pounds. The goal is to push the flywheel so that it rotates by simply leveraging your strength against it. By pushing once, it moves slightly. You realize that it will require multiple, consistent pushes to get it moving. After some pushing, it turns once. Then you keep pushing, and it turns again and again and again. Collins writes:

> Then, at some point—breakthrough! The momentum of the thing kicks in your favor, hurling the flywheel forward, turn after turn ... whoosh! ... its own heavy weight working for you. You're pushing no harder than during the first rotation, but the flywheel goes faster and faster. Each turn of the flywheel builds upon the work done earlier, compounding your investment of effort. A thousand times faster, then ten thousand, then a hundred thousand. The huge heavy disk flies forward, with almost unstoppable momentum.

> Now suppose someone came along and asked, "What was the one big push that caused this thing to go so fast?"

> You wouldn't be able to answer; it's just a nonsensical question. Was it the first push? The second? The fifth? The hundredth? No! It was all of them added together in an overall accumulation of effort applied in a consistent direction. Some pushes may have been bigger than others, but any single heave—no matter how large—reflected a small fraction of the entire cumulative effective upon the flywheel.[1]

The same is true in churches that have produced small groups that are currently experiencing MissioRelate. They don't stand up and announce that they will change the church by mobilizing everyone in a new small group program. Instead, leaders invest their energy in the right places to produce tangible results that reveals the power of being a part of a community on mission. They recognize that moving the MissioRelate flywheel will take time (in some cases a few years). They keep at it, pushing forward in little ways that only produces small results at first . . . and they celebrate those small results and even the turtle-slow pace of the process. They have learned something very valuable: this is God's way of building MissioRelate momentum.

After nearly 20 years of working with churches and small groups, I've observed that normal groups are often found in churches looking for the magical small group strategy that will make everything fall into place at once, within a budget cycle, or a school year. But those whose groups are moving out in mission started slow, kept at it, and have learned that consistent leverage creates movement. In contrast to flywheel effect, Collins observed a contrasting pattern in companies that were not able to implement new ideas or lead people to align around a vision. He writes:

> Instead of a quiet deliberate process of figuring out what needed to be done and then simply doing it, the comparison companies frequently launched new programs—often with great fanfare and hoopla aimed at "motivating the troops"—only to see the programs fail to produce sustained results. They sought the single defining action, the grand program, the one killer innovation, the miracle moment that would allow them to skip the arduous buildup stage and jump right to breakthrough. They would push the flywheel in one direction, then stop, change course, and throw it in a new direction—and then they would stop, change course, and throw it into yet another direction.[2]

To see a movement of missional group life develop in our churches, we must consider how to best apply a little leverage to the flywheel and then go about it quietly. We don't need any new programs, fanfare, or grand announcements about how small groups will change the life of our churches.

applying leverage to the right places

Our modern questions about success, group growth, ways to close the back door, and strategies to survive through the ups and downs of overseeing small groups leads us to put pressure on the wrong things. We end up running from one small flywheel to the next, thinking that we are generating movement when all we are doing is generating activity and extra work. Within the normal small group experience, people might believe everything about orthodox Christianity and mentally embrace the life of the church. Examine their lifestyle and you'll see it is formed more by the patterns of everyday church life than by the ways of God. Parker Palmer puts it this way:

> Churches, for example, ask members to affirm certain religious beliefs and the mission those beliefs imply. But rarely are churches intentional about naming—let alone asking members to commit themselves to—the relational norms and practices that would support their beliefs and mission. As a result, the relationships within many churches are shaped more by the norms of secular culture than by those of the religious tradition.[3]

If we want to develop ways of relating in groups that results in mission, then we must look at what and how we are applying the pressure. While reading the works of the small group prophets I wrote about earlier, I realized that they applied pressure quite differently than we do today. Let me list five strong contrasts that stood out to me:

• Their primary concern was not on church growth, the number of groups, or what percentage of the church was in groups. "A church of groups" was not the end goal, but a means for accomplishing God's greater mission. They had a vision for the redemption of creation and for empowering people to have a role in this redemption. Groups assisted them in this endeavor, and groups would often grow as a result of their focus. But there is little talk about how many groups, how people join groups, or other statistical issues.

• They maintained a keen focus on the quality of group life. They were looking for the kind of life that reflected the kingdom of God as represented by Jesus. These were not just study groups that met once per week or twice a month. They were groups that knew they had a call to be salt and light in the midst of the world. It was a radical call, one where Vice Presidents of large corporations were challenged to put feet to their faith by helping people dry out from long-term heroine use.

• These prophets were not afraid to "draw a line in the sand" and release those who would not enter the radical call to missional life. They did not water down the vision in order to pacify tithing members. They let the traditional churches in the neighborhood care for those who did not want to go deeper.

• They trained. And then they trained. And then they trained some more. They knew that such a vision for the church was radically different and it would not come naturally to their church members. They knew that if it was to be practiced, training was crucial. Their extensive member training processes raised the expectations of those involved. Then, they mentored people in the practical means of putting the training into practice. This produced powerful leaders who were anxious to lead.

• They experimented. They did not write about the need to find a structure or model for the next church, or one that could be packaged and sold to others. In their own way, each implied that the church should not go from one static form to the next static form called "small groups." They were using small groups to experiment with different ideas of being God's people out in front of a watching world.

To summarize, the leaders in these churches emphasized and focused on a different set of priorities. Most of the talk about small groups today focuses on finding the right strategy, which is a completely different animal. From my perspective, there are two places where we need to rethink how we apply this leverage. The first, obviously, is in small groups, house churches, cell groups, or whatever you call them. To this end, I wrote *Missional Small Groups* (Baker, 2010). This book is written for small group leaders, and even small group members, so that they can more clearly see the need and learn how to do it.

The second is not as obvious and often overlooked. It relates to how pastors, staff, small group champions and key unpaid supporters of group life leverage their energy. The following chapters will provide you with an imagination for and practical insights into what needs to be done and how to go about it in a simple, quiet way.

The chapters of Part 1 conclude with a reflective prayer exercise that is the same for each of these first four chapters. Most of the time we read to gain information. That is good. But I also want to encourage you to listen to the Spirit and your own responses to what you have read. I invite you to stop at the end of these chapters and go through this simple prayer guide and see what you discover that might be different.

On the next page, take time to reflect and journal about what you've just read. Look back over the chapter, identify things that stood out to you, and note them. Find the things with which you agree and those with which you don't. Mark them. Slowly review anything that challenges you or encourages you. Pray over those words. Write down what you sense the Spirit is speaking to you. Pray what you sense. Write down those prayers. Whatever you do, don't turn the page without pausing to ask God what he's saying to you right now.

missiorelate
*An experience with others and God
that makes a difference in the world*

the four stories of group life

Reflecting on my experience as a group leader, pastor, trainer, and consultant, I realized that different churches might adopt the same model of group structures—using the same training, the same oversight system, the same language, the same materials to give the groups, and the same level of priority in the church—but the lived experience within those churches would vary.

While reading the last chapter of Craig Van Gelder's book, *The Ministry of the Missional Church,* I had an epiphany. In a matter of minutes, my imagination about groups—whether called a cell group, house church, task group, missional community, or by any other name—shifted so dramatically that I had to rethink almost everything I believed and taught about groups. I'm not saying that I had to throw out all that I had previously known about groups. Instead, this shift changed everything about how I perceived what I knew.

In his book, Van Gelder identifies four different kinds of change people experience in life or in an organization. They are Improvement, Adjustment, Revision, and Re-creation. When I applied these four kinds of change to small group experiences, I discovered that groups tell four different stories with the way they live. These are not prescriptive patterns for group life given to those groups as labels. Instead, these are stories that describe the lived realities that groups experience. In my opinion, we have enough training and resources on the various ways to organize groups. We need resources that will help us navigate and lead people through the realities of life as they live these stories. The first two stories depict normal group experience while the third and fourth stories describe missional life (MissioRelate).

Personal Improvement

This is the small group experience where individuals participate because it is personally beneficial. The people involved are either drawn to a topic or to a group of people like themselves, and participation is high until it becomes inconvenient. Nothing in their personal life is required to change to participate in this kind of group. Quite the opposite is true: They expect their personal lives to be enriched from the "goods and services" provided by the small group experience. In *Missional Small Groups*, I illustrated how these stories might play out as a testimony. I've included them here as well to illustrate my explanations. Here's the first for Personal Improvement:

> We get together because life is tough in this world and we need a few friends. It is not always convenient for us to meet every week, but we do meet when we can. Usually we meet in short six- or seven-week periods or we meet a couple times a month. We get together, talk a bit about God or study the Bible, and share what is going on at work and in our family. I am not sure that we are close, but it is good to have a place where we can share a little about what is going on in our lives. Being in my small group has improved my life.[1]

Lifestyle Adjustment

This story is a continuation of the first. The group is viewed as beneficial, and therefore the group members are willing to adjust their life schedules to prioritize the attendance of a weekly or biweekly meeting. There is usually a longer-term commitment to group membership, but not much more than that. In fact, this story usually plays out in such a way that small group members attend meetings until they hit a time of conflict or struggle in the relationships within the group. While they adjust their lifestyle to prioritize a regularly scheduled small group meeting, they typically do not adjust their lives to make room to work through relational issues unearthed within a group. As a result, they either stop attending; attend meetings but in a way that is disengaged; or look for another similar group comprised of people with more compatible views and personalities. Here's how the description might sound in a much more lived way:

> This group has become a priority to us. We have adjusted our sched-
> ules to meet together at least every other week, but usually we meet
> weekly. In our meetings, we either study the sermon preached by
> our pastor or use a Bible study guide that we all find personally
> beneficial. We truly enjoy each other's presence, and we put a high
> priority on the group and the members in the group. We even do
> something social once each month. We rise to the occasion when
> someone has a need, and there is a sense that we are friends.[2]

Relational Revision

While the move from the first story to the second was a continuous progression, the move to this third is discontinuous. This story requires intentional practice. The facts are clear: the habits of the average person in North America are so contrary to a life of mutual love and self-sacrifice that if a group does not choose to practice a distinctively Christian way of life, nothing radical or kingdom-like will be experienced. The Relational Revision story is only told as a group develops a new set of rhythms, like a person might do when first learning to play the guitar. Hours of intentional practice are required. Here is where a group discovers distinctively Christian practices such as:

- Worship
- Encountering the presence of God together
- Communion
- Hospitality
- Mutual generosity
- Making time for each other
- Entering the neighborhood

I presented this information to 60 people at a Lutheran church where 40% of the crowd was over 55 years of age. I have never been able to communicate well with that demographic, but when I presented the four stories to them and explained the importance of Relational Revision in depth and how it prepares a group for mission, they expressed a keen sense of interest. When people clearly understand the reality that they have to learn how to practice the rhythms of missional life *together*, something within them resonates with this story. Most people inherently know that gathering for a small group meeting will not automatically result in a radical missional life. Something within us compels us to learn how to do this. A person might relate their Relational Revision story in this way:

Our group has a weekly meeting, but I am not sure that you would call it a *meeting* in the formal sense of the word. When we get together, it is the culmination of the rest of the week when we have been *in* one another's lives. It is a time of sharing what God has been doing, praying for each other, and talking about how God is using us in our everyday lives. Yes, we do have a weekly lesson, but the leader usually only asks one or two questions from it.

The most important part of our group, however, is not the meeting; it is how we are connected the other six days of the week. I have never been part of a group in which people are so willing to sacrifice time and energy for one another. And this connectedness actually spills out into our neighborhood. It seems like we are always interacting with, praying for, and serving people who live near us. And in some ways, they are just as much a part of our group as those of us who call ourselves *Christians*.

I am not sure how I was able to do life before having this group. This might sound a bit utopian, but it is far from it. Sometimes it is hard. Recently, we have had to wrestle with some relational conflict and hurt feelings. In the past I would have run away from such encounters, but not this time. It was not easy, but we pressed through. We are still learning what it means to be God's family.[3]

Missional Re-creation

As groups begin to practice these rhythms and gain proficiency—much like a novice guitar player will begin to expand her horizons beyond the notes on the page—a group will explore new ways of creative existence. They will engage the neighborhood and determine needs, meet those needs, and as a result, that experience will change how they exist as a group. Some will develop into house churches of 50. Others meet in groups of five meeting at a coffee shop. Others will adopt a home for mentally challenged individuals. And still others will gather around a family that lives in a mindset of poverty and walk with them into a new way of thinking and living. The key is not the form that it takes, but the maturity of living out the practices that are introduced in Relational Revision. Missional Re-creation flows out of a set of practices into an unpredictable structural future. Here is how it might be described:

We have developed a way of connecting with each other and God that has resulted in some rather unpredictable developments. Two couples and a single person in our group live within walking distance of each other. As a group, we decided to adopt their neighborhood. We started with a block party. At first it was hard because no one knew us, but after that first party, we created a small presence in the community. Then one person started a summer children's Bible study. As she got to know the neighbors and their needs, we began to pray. Now we have come around a single mom who has three kids, and we include her as much as we can in the life of the group. She has yet to fully understand who Jesus is, but we feel led to embrace her and the kids and see what God does in her life.[4]

the radical differences between the stories

The stories of Relational Revision and Missional Re-creation speak to what it means to be missional small groups that are trying to make a difference in this world. But let me be quite clear: there is no missional small group strategy or structure. The last two are illustrative of a missional *story*. They are so because when we live according to this story we are learning to live out ways of the kingdom of God. We are also recognizing the broader culture is a lived story and that it is not shaped by the kingdom of God. To be a community on mission means that a group of people are living a distinctive kingdom story in the midst of people who don't live that way.

By contrast, when we live out the stories of Personal Improvement and Lifestyle Adjustment we fail to recognize the difference between the story of the kingdom and our part in that story and the story of the world around us. As a result, the story of the broader culture sneaks into our lives as the people of God and we settle for less than what God has for us. This might sound judgmental, but if there is the chance that the primary ways that we think about small groups in North American don't measure up to what God has for us, then don't you think that we need to at least consider the possibility of something else? (Please stick with me through the end of this chapter on this thought. I do think that God moves through and uses the first two stories in the church today.) The chart below can be used to demonstrate the differences between the four stories.

The Story	Personal Improvement	Lifestyle Adjustment	Relational Revision	Missional Recreation
Lived Experience	Better Self	Surface-level Friendship	Contrast Society	Organic Mission
Focus	Me	Church	We	Neighborhood
Connection to Larger Church	Individual	Assimilation	Equipping	Creating & Involving
Cost	Easy in/ Easy Out	Meeting Attendance	Accountability	Radical Sacrifice
Goal	Connections	Close Back Door	Establish ways of Mission	Engagement with the Neighborhood
Discipleship	Event-centered	Curriculum Driven	Intentional Practices	Life-on-Life Mentoring
Evangelism	Invite to Chuch Events	Group Meeting	Relationships	In Neighborhood
Common Form of Groups	Short-term	Semester Groups Ongoing Groups	Groups Doing Practices	Organic Groups that take many forms

(Note: The following paragraphs are stated rather bluntly for the sake of clarity. Please forgive me if what I'm about to share seems judgmental. I just find that providing the following information is helpful to make a clear distinction between the stories.)

In the first two stories, community is squarely attractional. If the group is made up of the right people; or the leader does a good job leading the study; or the people one meets in these groups are friendly, then participation will be strong. From these stories' motivational perspective, getting the group meetings "right" is foundational for success. And, making these groups work is rooted in a desire to meet people's spiritual needs.

Churches that promote the *Personal Improvement* story emphasize groups in which people naturally desire to participate. For busy people, they create once-a-month groups. For people who fear commitment, short-term groups are the answer. For independent types, they are invited to start any kind of group they want. The focus lies on what the individuals in a church desire.

Lifestyle Adjustment groups focus on moving people into a meeting structure or closing the back door. It is an enfolding system. The focus lies on how the church can gather and keep people connected. Usually this story is heavily dependant upon a recruitment strategy so that there are enough groups for people to join. One might say that it is programmatic in nature.

Before you assume that I am deeming the first two stories as irrelevant, worthless, or even carnal, I am not. I clearly see a role for these two stories in most church situations in the West. I am thankful for and have learned much from those who have taught and written books and curriculum to help groups live out these two stories. In chapter 18, I will demonstrate a process that takes advantage of these two stories that helps people move beyond the "me" or even the "church" focus and into an organic way of being a missional "light" right where they live.

we are called to be a "light to the nations"

We usually apply the mandate found in Isaiah to taking the message of the gospel to unreached people groups in far-flung places. This is indeed part of the meaning. When God called Israel to be a "light," he was not challenging them to send missionaries throughout the world to plant churches. He called them to a mission as his people into his world to live in his way. They were his chosen people who were called to live his way, to be a sign to the rest of the world of what it means to live in relationship with God.

The focus of *Relational Revision* is about learning how to be this light and how to live rhythms that fit God's mission in this world. These groups form communities where people learn to be God's light in the midst of the darkness. They are not just groups set up for Bible study or for retention in a growing congregation. They are groups that empower people to discover God's ways and live out God's story.

When these groups move into the *Missional Re-creation* story, we discover people who have embodied these new rhythms. Mission has become a rooted value or deeply motivational part of their life. As a result, the forms that their groups take and the structures that develop will often be creative and unique. Rather than following some predetermined pattern handed to them by leadership or what they find in a popular book on small groups, they have learned to play missional music and that music forms a creative and unique rhythm.

As I have taught these four stories to people from all kinds of church traditions, most readily state that their group experiences have more in common with the Lifestyle Adjustment story than any other. Most were like me when I first saw the four stories: I did not know what to do to help people change this reality. But admitting that we don't know is the first step to learning something that might change everything.

On the next page, take time to reflect and pray through what you read. Look back over the chapter and identify things that stood out to you. Find the things with which you agree and those with which you don't. Mark them. Slowly re-read anything that seemed to challenge you or encourage you. Then pray over those words. Write down what you sense the Spirit is speaking to you. Pray what you sense. Write down those prayers in the space provided on the next page.

missiorelate
An experience with others and God
that makes a difference in the world

why do we need these stories?

When I first started as the Community Pastor at my church, our annual retreat was already planned. Paul Eddy, our teaching pastor, was invited to lead the central part of the training. Paul is a professor of theology at Bethel University with a specialty in how theology intersects with a narrative reading of the Bible (allowing the big picture story of the Bible to shape one's theology). As a result, the focus of that weekend was not highly practical in nature . . . something for which I am now thankful.

What he shared that weekend was overwhelmingly significant. It took me five years to see the depth of its value, but I've found that most of the richest stuff in the world does not come to us quickly. I've discovered that the perspective he taught that day opens up a new universe to hear the missional story within a biblical framework. But even more so, it gives us a tool to understand the story of normal groups and why simply adopting a new vision called "missional small groups" won't actually change anything at all.

If we are going to change the story of our groups from the normal experience to something that resembles Relational Revision or Missional Re-creation, we must get inside the story that shapes our lives. This is the story about personal identity and how we view ourselves.

how the ancients knew who they were

Who are you? When someone asks you this question, how do you respond? Most likely it is very different than how someone from ancient Israel imagined their identity. In fact, every culture prior to the present, modern Western culture was shaped by the imagination below.

If you were born during the times of Abraham, Isaac and Jacob, you would have been shaped by a conversation between these three elements. God (or in the case of other peoples, "a god") was crucial to a person's self-perception. Who they worshipped shaped who they were. For us moderns this is not that hard to understand. But the next two are.

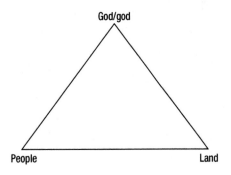

Ancients were shaped by belonging to a specific people, tribe, or family.
Great Western thinkers have shaped our imagination and we view ourselves as a *thinking* individual, a *feeling* individual, or an *acting* individual. In today's world, "who I am" is all about me and how I would characterize myself. In the ancient world, a person's identity could never be separated from the question, "To whom do you belong?"

Pre-moderns were shaped by the land in which they lived.
They were "place" people who were very rooted in a sense of physicality. This is not the case for most people today, as we are "space" people who think in terms of a huge gulf lying between our physical experiences and our spiritual experiences. Therefore, our personal identity is an abstract "mind" issue that supposedly remains consistent regardless of where we live or with whom we share our life.

In the ancient world, a person like Abraham saw himself as being defined by the God he worshipped, the people around him to whom he belonged and the land on which he lived. When God invited Abraham to leave his family and land, he entered a time of identity crisis that would reshape everything he knew about himself and God. But God did not invite Abraham into an individualistic, "spiritual" experience. Instead, God promised to establish a new people and a new land through Abraham. God was establishing a new triangle.

applying the triangle to the modern church

When I first heard Paul Eddy teach on this triangle of personal identity, I thought to myself "That's a nice history lesson, but what do we do with it today when no one actually thinks in these terms in our churches, much less in our neighborhoods?" But I could not escape the concept. I found it reinforced in the writings of Old Testament scholars like Christopher Wright and Walter Brueggeman. I considered how we live in community and the individualism that pervades our culture and wondered if this triangle has anything to do with why small groups remain so normal in the West, even though we are not lacking in passion, creativity, or resources about how to do groups.

Then I re-read and wrestled with the works of Lesslie Newbigin, a man who is generally considered the father of missional thinking in the West.

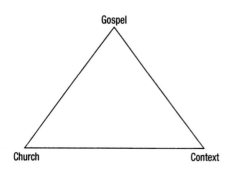

Newbigin spoke of a slightly different but corresponding triangle that highlighted a way to apply this ancient "trialogue" today (see diagram at left).

As Newbigin returned to England after over 30 years of service as a missionary to India, he found himself in the same role in his home country. The church as he knew it was no longer feasible. To be an effective home missionary, he did not think in terms of what kind of church or small group structure would be needed to reach the West. Instead, he thought of it in terms of a conversation between how we speak about the gospel in the context in which

47

we live. Out of this new paradigm, he found church life or "peoplehood."

In reality, this three-way conversation is already occurring in our version of Western Christianity. For many in North America, the gospel is a simple message of good news to individuals so that they can experience personal salvation and then go to heaven when they die. Salvation is primarily shaped by a vertical imagination about "me" and God. As I reflect on the endless salvation sermons I have heard through the years, the central point was always, "Are you ready to go to heaven?" Or, "What is the status of your personal relationship with God?" In other words, my imagination about salvation was focused on being saved personally from the penalty of sin.

Now don't hear me wrong, I'm not saying that salvation is not about heaven or a personal relationship with God, but there is so much more to it than that. I am glad that I am free from the penalty of sin, but the Bible also talks about the fact that we are "being saved" and that God's salvation plan is about the redemption of all creation, not just a bunch of individuals who possess a one-on-one, individual relationship with God.

our view of salvation shapes our understanding of "context" and "church"

As I said earlier, when we think of our physical experience we don't normally connect that with our life with God. God deals in terms of things that are non-physical. So where we live, what we do for a living, how we spend our time, and our hobbies are personal choices that have little to no bearing on our spiritual lives. As long as we are "saved," attend a church regularly, have an inner personal relationship with Jesus and are moral people, then it seems that we can live our lives however we choose. (I realize I am overstating the case, but I do so to make a point.) Our personal spirituality is spoken about in terms of our personal time with God, Bible reading, and a commitment to prayer . . . all inner world experiences that are not related to how we do life in physical terms.

Over the past few years, there has been a massive focus on financial stewardship within the church. One voice from this movement has developed excellent material to help people get their finances in order. But the motivation used to promote this financial program is to put aside money and invest it in such a way that one can live like no one else *and* retire early. Of course, scripture is used to support each point, but one could remove the scriptures and it would remain sound as personal financial advice. But there is something lacking. There is nothing in this popular material about the call to live simply, sacrificing for one another, sharing one's resources in community, or embracing the poor. When it comes to money, these pursuits seem to be the focus of the Bible. Conversely, the church's most popular teaching on the subject seems to promote an individualistic, middle-class suburban set of values, using the Bible to support these new conclusions.

Let's turn our attention to the church part of the triangle. If the gospel is about getting saved from guilt so that we can go to heaven and create a deeper spiritual experience with God, the logical conclusion for the church is to become a gathering of individuals who exercise their preference to attend a specific place of worship. One person prefers a big church with lots of programs. Another prefers the preaching of an intellectual pastor. Some prioritize a smaller church that is more like a big family. However the choices are made, people typically conceive the ideal church as providing the four "specials" to meet their spiritual needs. The four "specials" are the *special meetings* (church services with singing, some liturgy, and preaching) that meet at *special times* (11:00 a.m. on Sunday) at *special places* (church buildings) led by *special people* (usually addressed as Reverend, Brother, or Father). As a result of the common way we do the three-way conversation between gospel, context, and church, our churches—or at least the expectations that people have of churches—are relegated to being providers of spiritual goods and services.

How do we change this?

This is a huge challenge. Over the last 25 years, church leaders have spoken and written about current issues facing the church. One of the more popular thoughts is to revert back to a New Testament model. It is obvious to me that the early church's four "specials" were vastly different than the modern church. The meetings were special not because early Christians went to a service, but because they met in unofficial ways, usually over a meal where everyone participated. The time was special because there was no specific "spiritual" time; they met whenever and as often as they needed. The special place was homes, courtyards, guildhalls, riverbanks, or wherever they could gather. And the leaders were special because they were facilitators of ministry between everyone instead of a few special people.

Many Christians today—including myself in my former days—elevate the first century church as the ideal to which we all should strive. However, I find no ideal or perfect practice prescribed for churches of future generations to follow in the New Testament beyond principles by which to live. Instead, what I find in the early church was far from idyllic. I find back-biting, factions, abuse by leadership, and even immorality. But this isn't the main issue and it should not be the main focus of this discussion. It's impossible for modern-day North Americans to return to the status of a new movement forming within the unique context of the Roman Empire. We have 20 centuries of church history that have shaped the western world, even for those who never participated in church life. We have dead churches that have communicated that the gospel of Jesus Christ lacks power. We have television evangelists that promote a version of the gospel that turns off many believers and potential believers. My bottom line is that our situation and our context is not that of first century Corinth, Galatia, or Ephesus. We can learn from the early church and work to change the specials, but we must also deal with our reality.

Even though this is the case, many of us still think that we can just change the structure and somehow gain far better results. We teach on developing organic house churches and then parcel them out to meet in homes. We change how we do church, but it ends up that we remain stuck in the same normal stories. Structurally it might have more in common with what is found in the primitive churches in the New Testament, but what is experienced is not that different.

You may think that this doesn't apply to you because you're not interested in abandoning what you're doing today for a house church, but the same assumption can be transferred to modern churches looking for improvement. There's a strong temptation to develop a vision for "missional small groups" and then get people involved. People may join one of these newly labeled groups, but their story will be normal. Calling a group "missional" won't change the story of the participants. People join these groups within the same imagination about the gospel, church, and context that I described earlier. The small group is a place where I can reinforce my personal experience of salvation. It has little to do with my way of life in the real world . . . and as soon as this group does not fulfill my needs, I'll find another or abandon group life because it's not personally satisfying my current need or desire.

change the triangle

It does not matter how radical your vision may be for small groups or house churches or missional communities, whatever you want to call it. I don't care how much teaching you offer on how to do church in more biblical ways. If you don't help people reframe their view of personal identity, which is rooted in their Western individualized version of the gospel, you will continue to be stuck with groups who never go beyond normal.

To move people into MissioRelate, you must change the way you live the triangle. (Notice I chose the word "live" and I did not use "think about" or "consider"). The way we live is directly connected to the way we think about the three corners of the triangle.

Our theology shapes our daily experience
A nutshell version of the Gospel (the good news) could be stated as, "Jesus rose from the dead." We have said much about Jesus' death and now with all the research on the historical Jesus there is much to say about his life. But the component that changes everything about his life and death is the fact that he

51

did not remain in a grave. Without the resurrection, Jesus is just normal.

With the resurrection, Jesus opened the door to the restoration of all of creation. My personal experience of salvation is only a part of the sweeping salvation plan of everything. Because of this, we can emphasize the ongoing truth that we are being saved from the power of sin in the current realities of life. This means that the gospel has "right now" ramifications for how we live. We don't have to wait for deliverance from the presence of sin to experience the gospel.

This also has implications for community. There is good news that God is saving Western Christians from our individualism and our self-obsession. The move from normal group life to MissioRelate is not rooted in what we do. It is based in the fact that God is at work in this world. By the Spirit of God, we are empowered to make choices that abandon normal for something much greater and more transformational.

When we move into the context corner, we move beyond personal spirituality and embrace God who has embraced us in our everyday secular world. We can imagine how our life with Christ and one another engages our lives at work, play, and family. We move beyond "the me and God" experience to attain eyes that see what God is doing on our streets, in our neighborhoods, and in our friends. This is an earthy spirituality that sees God at work in all of life.

When the triangle is changed and embraced, we can now consider questions about church and what that might look like. We can finally move beyond personal choices where we seek a church to meet our personal preferences. Here, we learn to practice church in such a way that engages our real lives in our specific context. We don't go to our context with a predetermined structure of how we do church as if there is a universally valid approach. Instead, we embody the gospel, listen to what is going on in our context, and together discover what it means to be the church.

As church leaders, when we change the triangle and help people reframe how they perceive themselves, we have the potential to change our small group story. How we facilitate this change is the focus of Part 2 of this book. Between those pages and the ones that follow, I want to demonstrate how one's perspective of the four stories changes some commonly held small group teachings.

On the next couple of pages, take some time to reflect and pray through what you read. Look back over the chapter and identify things that stood out to you. Find the things with which you agree and those with which you don't. Mark them. Slowly re-read anything that seemed to challenge you or encourage you. Then pray over those words. Write down what you sense the Spirit is speaking to you. Pray what you sense. Write down those prayers in the space provided on the next pages.

missiorelate
*An experience with others and God
that makes a difference in the world*

how the four stories change everything

I have a new iPhone and I love it. It's wonderful to have my computer, web access, my calendar, and my emails in my pocket. I can read books on it. I've even written part of this book by tapping my fingers on the little screen. This gizmo also gives me constant access to Twitter, Facebook, and the blogs I follow. Oh yeah. I can make phone calls with it too! In many ways, the iPhone has "changed everything" just as Apple's promotional tag states.

In fact, it's fun to stand in lines now. I can read people's ideas as they ponder them aloud in their "tweets." I'll admit it's a bit hard for me to tweet. I like to think through an idea thoroughly before I put it out there for public consumption. But we live in a new world of dialogue and conversation. No one person can claim to have the corner on the truth. We live in a humbling time of continual learning and discovery. The day of the sole guru for a particular industry is gone.

In a down moment a few days ago, I was reading a series of comments on my iPhone about various things regarding small groups and it was frustrating. Comments were being posted to which I responded, "Really? You actually believe that's the truth?" Then my frustration blossomed into anger as I realized how many other people were reading these half-truths and myths without a challenge. My thoughts ranged from a knee-jerk "That's just stupid!" to a humble "I used to say the same thing" or a conclusive "That's actually true if all you are looking to develop is more normal group stories."

I did not want to think this way. Many of these statements were being made or have been made by close friends of mine. When I stopped and thought about it deeply, I realized that I had embraced what they wrote in the past, but the four stories had changed everything for me. It had taken me on a paradigm shift and opened my eyes to see something about each of the statements that I never saw before.

This chapter identifies a few statements that have become common fare amongst small group teachers, followed by an explanation of how the four stories have given me a different perspective.

"The goal is to become a church of small groups."

My friends Bill Donahue and Russ Robinson made the vision for small groups compelling in their book *Becoming a Church of Small Groups*. I am grateful for what they wrote and how the church has benefited from their teaching. And to be quite honest, my concern is not with that book in particular. I am more concerned with what church leaders have done with the word "of." This word has been used to zero in on identifying the percentage of people in our churches who are involved in groups. Is it 80, 100, or 120 percent? These are the numbers that are touted as marks of success. Or, do we have more common numbers like 33 percent as Joseph Myers reports in his books? Numbers of groups and percentages of congregational participation take a back seat when you view these statistics through the lens of the four stories. In this new paradigm, we care far more about the depth of spiritual life exchange found in groups.

Every year, *Outreach* magazine identifies and features the largest churches and the fastest growing churches in the United States. My perennial response is, "Who cares?" I don't care how many people attend worship services or the number of satellite campuses in a mega church. I'm far more interested in the life that these people lead. Don't hear me being frustrated because my church is not on that list. Our church is big enough and successful enough by any standard, but we are not content with the kind of life that we see today.

A friend of mine was in a gathering that brought together the best and brightest small groups pastors from the nation's largest small group churches.

As he spoke with one staff pastor with hundreds and hundreds of groups under his care, the pastor quietly confessed that he has no idea what actually goes on in his groups. Is this good enough? Are we satisfied with just being a church of groups if we have no idea what's genuinely going on in those groups? Don't get me wrong. Good things can and do come out of these groups, but there must be more.

"Traditional bible studies, task groups, and interest groups serve no purpose."

Some might assume that the only kinds of groups that I see as having value are groups that are living out the vision of MissioRelate. I used to teach this very thing. I thought that the only thing we needed were groups that were living out the ultimate vision of dynamic community on mission. Anything less was compromise. And my friends Ralph Neighbour and Joel Comiskey—along with all those from the cell church world that have read some of my previous writings—might think I have made a grave compromise because I no longer promote this sentiment.

The stories have helped me see things differently. Instead of focusing on a specific small group type to carry out the vision for the church, I have four stories. And when I see that groups are not living out the vision of MissioRelate, I don't berate them or shut them down. I help people identify their story and take steps to move toward something different. In other words, I no longer think in either/or terms. Task groups, short-term campaign groups, Bible studies and even things like a volleyball group can be used to help groups along the journey of moving from one story to another. The key is that we have to be clear that group involvement is not the ultimate goal. Being on a journey and taking steps toward God's call to move from one story to the next must be our goal.

"Groups build biblical community."

I know I am nitpicking the use of the word "build" but it's worth mentioning here. People use this word because they want to train people in the practical and positive things that they can do to contribute to biblical community. For this reason, I applaud the use of this word. Of course, our actions can either positively contribute to community or negatively deter it.

In the West, especially in America and even more so in evangelical churches, people have a practical bent. They want to know what they can do so they will know what God wants them to do. Too many times the pressure for obedience is put squarely on the shoulders of people and they hear, "Do something!" However, I have found that every time I try to make community happen—me building it with a new program or initiative—very few respond. Relationships just don't work that way. Think about a young man who falls for a girl and tries to force her to like him because he so badly likes her. I remember one time I met with a couple of guys at a coffee shop and I wanted to intentionally build connections with them. So I told them of my intentions. The look on their faces told me to back off.

The four stories have shown me how community is an experience that we discover as we walk together on a journey. Yes, I can do things that help us move along in our journey, but I'm just not sure how much I build it. This is the reason that Lyman Coleman, the great small groupologist who influenced countless churches, called his ministry Serendipity. Something is "serendipitous" when one discovers something desirable by accident. Community is a wonder, like that of the pearl in Jesus parable. I'm not satisfied with what I can build myself. We must learn to discover it together.

"Nothing fosters community more than being on mission together."

I love the word "foster" because it speaks to how we contribute to the discovery of biblical community. And I do think that being on mission together has the ability to foster community. But to say "nothing fosters community more than being on mission" is an overstatement. It sounds good, but it just doesn't line up with reality.

A colleague of mine argued this point very strongly a few years back. She was adamant that a group that is serving together would experience more community than one that is not. But I have known numerous small groups that I don't want out in the community serving others. They just don't have much of the kind of life that is naturally contagious or organically demonstrates God's love. They would be going through the motions of mission, but they have not learned the life of love that empowers a group to have something to give others. Their efforts would have no lasting fruit.

I used to think that giving a group some kind of challenge to serve outside of themselves would help them shift from being a normal group to something like the Relational Revision story. But the reality is that they only did the task and then came back to the group meeting, carrying on their lives as it was before. I'm glad they performed the task. Their group meetings were better off because they served together, but their story did not suddenly shift as a result of performing the task.

In order to move into MissioRelate, most groups need to be equipped and prepared for life in the new story. They don't easily or quickly shift over by waving a magic wand of getting involved in some kind of service project or outreach program. A group filled with stressed, overworked suburbanites will not suddenly change their ways and become missional because they served people at the local homeless shelter a couple of Saturdays in a row. I don't believe that people who make this statement think that a service event will instantly transform a group, but too often that is the way the statement is interpreted.

"Giving your groups outreach projects or ideas promotes mission."

There is a common idea promoted by many pastors that groups can become missional if they only help them start reaching out. So they organize various outreach or social justice activities. These might range from simple acts such as passing out water on a hot day at the park or as involved as a church-wide project to build a playground in the neighborhood. The ideas and systems that church leadership can provide are only limited by the creativity of the leaders involved. Groups might commit to feeding the homeless on a monthly basis or participate in a moving ministry for those in need.[1]

I think ideas like these are good and I am not against them. But to call these acts of kindness "missional" is just replacing the term "outreach" or "evangelism" with a popular new term or label (missional). Doing things that are activist in orientation can help a group focus on outreach, but these activities can actually distract a group from becoming missional.

Being "missional" is different from doing something that *looks* missional. A missional small group is about embracing a way of life that makes a difference in the world, not just doing outreach, externally-focused activities for those not in the church. While the chart below overemphasizes the contrast, it illustrates the centrality of being over doing:

	Being	Doing
Focus of Mission	Group life	Outreach activities
Source of Mission	Overflow	Effort
Goal of Mission	Be a Blessing	Add people to group
Power of Mission	Love	Action
Key Trait of Mission	Conversations	Presentations

Being missional includes the doing, but when we emphasize the doing we create a "dog chasing its tail" effect. We get caught in the circle of doing without ever considering how we are being. Being missional is about developing a set of rhythms of love that stand in contrast to the world around us so that the love of God might flow through the community. This life of mission empowers the group for conversations instead of going out with answers and actions.

The four stories have opened my imagination to see that the shift from normal to missional is about who we are and not just what we do. I've participated in all kinds of outreach activities that have little impact on who we are as a community. We do something good and we seek to make an impact, but then we return to normal. Shifting a group from one story to the next is about deep change, requiring the group to rethink who they are, and not just what they do. I'll admit that sometimes outreach activities can help a group see the need for this fundamental or deep change, but if church leaders don't provide a process for entering into this deep change all they will have are the same old outreach activities that make very little difference in our world.

"There can be nothing that competes with the small group structure."
I used to make this statement with great conviction, but the four stories changed my perspective. I believe that the statement is completely true for people that are committed to groups that are focused on living out MissioRelate. More specifically, if people are going to enter into the story of Relational Revision or Missional Re-creation, then it is crucial to set them free from commitments to other ministries in the church. But the fact is that most people in our churches are not ready for this kind of life. I found that volunteering as a youth leader or singing in the choir is a lot more fun and actually more spiritually enlightening than many of my previous group experiences that are living out the stories of Personal Improvement or Lifestyle Adjustment. So why would I want to pull people away from these so-called competing areas of service or ministry?

Creating a "no-competition structure" from scratch (by planting a new church) is not difficult. In established churches, things will always be messy. Managing buildings, covering weekend services, and finding volunteers for the children and youth ministries is just messy ongoing work. Recently, the leadership of my church realized that many of our people build significant relationships with others by volunteering as ushers or in the children's ministry. But we had mistakenly told them that the only real way to live out community was through the small groups. We forced a "one-size-fits-all" strategy in a church with many current sizes and shapes. While the elevation of small groups above these other supportive programs bolstered numbers in our groups, it did not actually change the story that those groups of people were living out.

With an understanding of the four stories, we can see how there are many different ways that people can connect and live out the first two stories. But when they commit to something more than normal, then we must ask them to focus on living out a more radical story and not spread themselves too thinly.

"Goals for multiplication motivate people to grow their groups."
Statistical research has demonstrated that churches that set growth goals for groups are far more likely to grow in numbers of groups than those who don't. While it's hard to argue with statistics, my concern is the imagination

that a strong focus on multiplication goals creates within the people I lead. If we establish growth goals for our groups, the focus will lie on the *number* of groups we multiply, not the *kind* of groups we multiply. Plus, the story that our groups live together goes out the window altogether.

If we are going to lead people effectively, we must understand the stories that they currently live and respond with their best interest at heart, not the best interest of the small group model we've chosen. I've seen too many people in our groups who are struggling to keep their marriages together, to survive a tough job situation, or to keep their teenagers off drugs. Mandates surrounding multiplication goals do not meet these people at the point of need. Setting goals is the way pastors and leaders like to talk, but the people in our groups don't. I'm not saying that goals are unimportant. They are very important. But the goal is people not numbers of groups. If we set goals for loving people deeply, then we will hit our numeric goals in far more natural ways.

The four stories give us a different way to think about goals. Instead of multiplication of groups, we can establish goals for the kind of life we want to generate. We should strive to understand who the people are, the realities that they face, and set goals for creating groups that meet people at that point. For example, a church might learn that most of their current groups are living the story of Lifestyle Adjustment. The goal might be to find three groups who are ready to move beyond that and move into the story of Relational Revision. Even as groups begin to live out this new story, the goal is not simply to grow from three groups to five (or some other number we may establish). The goal is to understand how these groups are living out the mission—where they are strong and weak—and help them advance in that story. As people mature from one story to the next, they will be ready and willing to lead a new MissioRelate group.

I am convinced that if we live out MissioRelate, we won't have to worry about growth. We will engage our neighborhoods and demonstrate the love of Christ in attractive and compelling ways. Our goals should focus on the kind of life we lead. When we do this, the growth will take care of itself.

"The senior pastor must be the small group pastor."

This statement has been promoted going all the way back to David Yongii Cho in the 1970s. The belief is that if the senior pastor does not own the vision and promote it then it will be impossible to get a high percentage of the church into groups. I agree with this statement in more than just theory. In most cases, the senior pastor is the senior promoter. If he is not talking about group participation then people will opt out. And to take it a step further, if he is not actually participating in a group and sharing his personal experiences from the pulpit on a regular basis, people will not follow suit. One need only turn to the best-selling book *Creating Community* by Andy Stanley and my friend Bill Willits to find this. Andy has always been in groups and therefore he can promote group participation from his personal experience.

Once again, from the perspective of the four stories, things change. You cannot promote participation in Relation Revision or Missional Re-creation from the pulpit. You can talk about it. You can preach about it. You can even include testimonies from those who are living these stories. But when you depend upon promotion from the pulpit as a way to fill groups, the resulting stories will be those of Personal Improvement and Lifestyle Adjustment. There may be a few who are ready for more than normal groups, but most are not.

Why do I say this? Bill Beckham was my pastor for a few years in an experimental church in the early 1990s. He would say, "The way you get them is the way you keep them." By this he meant that if we attracted people into the church through relationships and sacrificial mission, they would continue on the journey with that same experience. So if our attraction was great pro-grams and entertaining services, we'd have to keep those going to keep them. I believe this is true. People can progress through the stories from normal to missional, but those who come on weekends looking for traditional church life initially want small groups that are going to follow suit. And those are the kinds of groups we can promote in our weekend services.

MissioRelate is promoted through exposure to communities who are living the group stories that go well beyond normal. New Christians are often more open to entering the MissioRelate story compared to established Christians.

Reach someone for Christ through a small group and they will be discipled through those relationships. Try to promote missional groups through weekend services and you will fill groups with people who may have good intentions and desire a missional lifestyle or value set, but they don't really understand the depth of the commitment. As a result, group life promoted from the pulpit alone will be watered down and get mired in normal group stories.

"Our model of group life is the most biblical."

This statement seems to have lost some steam over the last few years in some circles but in others it is more prevalent than ever. Let me give a few examples of how this is usually argued. Over the years, some have quoted Acts 2:42-46 and Acts 20:20 to support the small group/large group structure. They claim that these verses state that they met publicly and from house to house. Then, of course, they use the same verses to argue for meeting in houses, as opposed to church buildings, and for moving from house to house each week, instead of using host homes.

Others have found a hard and fast way to structure church leadership from Jethro's interaction to Moses in Exodus 18. On his father-in-law's suggestion, Moses established leaders of 1000s, 100s, 50s, and 10s. Then came those in the G-12 or "Groups of 12" camp who tossed that aside claiming that the Jethro model was for the Old Covenant and that the New Covenant should be structured around 12s. I actually heard a pastor from South America make this point in a seminar. My New Testament theology training almost caused me to jump out of my seat. (If you don't know what this is about, don't be concerned. Consider yourself lucky that you were not pulled into this foolish debate!)

Today there is another significant group influenced by authors that claim that the organic house groups were all that occurred in the New Testament … and anything more than that today is a perversion of God's dream for the church. In other words, we don't need preaching, large group meetings, or leadership oversight of groups. All we need is organic house groups. This is based on the assumption that since this is the way the first churches were organized, today's church should be no different.

The truth is that there is no magic in any structure. I've found simple churches (identified by a flat leadership structure) that claim to follow the pattern of the New Testament, yet live out the story of Lifestyle Adjustment. There is nothing automatically missional about participating in a simple organic house church versus traditional church structures. In fact, whenever we assume that any kind of change in structure will change our story, we fail to change anything that is genuinely important. The way we live will not necessarily change because we choose to meet differently. However, if we change our story we will have a valid and supportive reason to change our structure.

"We don't need small groups. Instead, we need mid-size missional communities."

There is another perspective that claims that small groups are too small to actually be missional. What is needed are groups of 20-50. Quite frankly, I am very sympathetic to this as you will see below. I encourage a lot of creative expressions of missional life.[2] However, where I grow concerned is the fact that people will jump on the new structure and miss the story that makes them missional. I do not think that the promoters of this form of missional life claim that their structure will produce mission. In fact, they do a great job of explaining the various elements that must be in place for missional life to occur. I just don't think that every context is the same. In some cases, small groups can be quite missional. In others, groups might find that networking together is the best option. And still others might find that a house church of 20-50 works very well. More important than any prescribed structure is the development of leaders who have the ability to discern what the Spirit is doing then respond to the question of form that MissioRelate story might take.

allow the four stories to change what you do

The chapters in the following pages speak to practical ways we can transition from one story to the next. Just keep in mind that we don't start living out the stories of MissioRelate because we've decided it's the right thing to do. Returning to the flywheel analogy, you won't find a business that does not want to make the flywheel spin and spin fast. But desire is not enough. A vision for a successful, financially sound business that exceeds normal expectations won't make it happen year after year. Companies that experience consistent yearly growth go well beyond the norm to make it happen and keep it happening. They fundamentally change how they operate and never become complacent, even when they experience success or movement.

If we are going to change the outcomes of our small groups from normal to MissioRelate, then we must change what we do. Einstein said, "Insanity is doing the same thing over and over again and expecting different results." If we want to see the stories of Relational Revision and Missional Re-creation told through our groups, then we must push the flywheel differently.

On the next page, take some time to reflect and pray through what you just read. Look back over the chapter and identify things that stood out to you. Find the things with which you agree and those with which you don't. Mark them. Slowly re-read anything that seemed to challenge you or encourage you. Then pray over those words. Write down what you sense the Spirit is speaking to you. Pray what you sense. Write down those prayers in the space provided on the next page.

part two

what we can do
to change everything

missiorelate
*An experience with others and God
that makes a difference in the world*

ask different questions

We have a choice. The story we tell with our lives and through our groups can be normal or MissioRelate. How we choose to live is based on the life rhythms we practice, which happens behind the scenes when no one is looking. For example, if you want to proficiently play the guitar, prepare yourself for hours of awkward sounding rhythms punctuated with raw fingertips for a number of months or even years. There is no magic formula for learning to play an instrument. You must apply the leverage of practicing your instrument of choice until it becomes second nature to pick it up and play beautiful music.[1]

If we want our groups to tell a distinctive MissioRelate story, we must learn to play the rhythms of missional community, which are different from the current reality for most individuals, small groups, and church organizations. I have found that the questions we ask about groups shape our rhythms and therefore shape where we leverage the flywheel. We must learn about and then ask a completely new set of questions that fit the rhythms of missional life if we want to see it come to fruition. Normal questions will not bring about radical change.

normal questions

In his book, *Community*, Peter Block writes about the kind of life that brings transformation to neighborhoods. He writes, "The small group is the unit of transformation and the container for the experience of belonging."[2] This transformation is both personal and societal. Throughout his book, he consistently makes a strong argument proving "authentic transformation does not occur by focusing on changing individuals" but by creating environments where small groups of people can generate an alternative future for the social fabric of a neighborhood. To put it in the language of Jesus, the kingdom of God comes through a group of people who are willing to embody the good news and manifest that good news in the everyday life of local neighborhoods.

Block opens the first chapter of his book with these words: "Social fabric is created one room at a time. It is formed from small steps that ask, 'Who do we want in the room?' and, 'What is the new conversation that we want to occur?'"[3] These questions generate conversations about creating an alternative future or a group of people who live in a distinctively different way compared to one's cultural norms. They are questions that require little communities to come up with their own answers instead of implementing a program that has been orchestrated from the top down or borrowed from a book from a mega church. In other words, these are questions that force groups to seek God and discover along the way what the Spirit is saying to the church.

As I mentioned, these questions are different from the questions most often asked when it comes to small group ministry. Church leaders often ask normal questions:

- How many groups does your church have?
- How many people are in groups?
- What percentage of your church is in groups?
- How many of your groups multiplied in the last year?
- How many new groups have formed in the last year?

Individual groups or group leaders are challenged with normal questions:

- How many people are in your group?
- How many people attended your meeting this week?
- How many people have you reached for Jesus?
- What is your plan for group multiplication?
- Who are you mentoring to be a future group leader?

When I first started working with churches to help them establish groups, these were the common or normal questions we asked. Specifically, we asked pastors to assess the health of their group *structure.* When coaching others and pastoring groups since that time, the answers to these questions created the statistics used to track progress or "success" as a small groups pastor. I learned how to develop charts, record data in spread sheets, and make reports to impress my bosses with numbers.

where normal questions lead us

I am not against group multiplication or moving a large percentage of a church to groups. But if these are our primary measurements of success in small group ministry, we will leverage the flywheel in ways that undermine mission. There are numerous ways to get lots of groups started and meet around topics that have nothing to do with God's kingdom. If the goal is to get all the people who attend a church on Sunday into a group during the week, then determining the interests of those people and establish groups around those interests is all that is required. Furthermore, one could answer all of the normal questions positively by creating groups that people want to attend without ever considering how they might be on mission in this world. Just poll the people to determine what individuals want. Then, announce biweekly groups. New people come to the church, survey the biweekly small group options, find an interest group, and sign up.

On paper, this looks great. New groups are springing up all the time. A large and increasing percentage of the people in the big group are now attending a small group as well. And best of all, people enjoy the small groups! Here's a harsh reality: most of these people are just *attending the meetings*. They show up after a long day to get to know the eight other people in the room with whom they've had no time to share life outside that meeting.

Meeting attendance does not make a group something that participates in the kingdom of God. Talking about the Bible or working through the latest Bible study material—risky words to put in print, but true nevertheless—does not mean that we are involved in a distinctively Christian activity. Meeting attendance and Bible discussion should lead to something far greater if we are going to be about what Jesus called the kingdom of God.

The new MissioRelate questions are radically different. Asking these new questions will determine the rhythms we practice because those questions shape our *imaginations*. The normal questions above actually limited our imagination and hindered us from seeing that which God wants to do through small group life in our time. We must think beyond the collection of data that fits nicely on a spreadsheet to justify the value of small groups to decision makers. We must embrace questions that will reshape the way we live in our culture and possibly how we do church.

missiorelate questions

I consulted a small church of 50 members in Pennsylvania that embarked upon a small group journey ten years before they contacted me for support. They hired me to assess why they were not growing. In our first discussions about their history, they shared the titles of books they initially read, promising spiritual and numeric growth, relational evangelism, and "success" if they launched small groups. A decade later, they remain a congregation of less than 50 but didn't know why they had not grown numerically.

During my initial visit, I found a few things they could do differently to grow larger in numbers. More than any other discoveries for improvement, I found that they were doing a lot of things right. There was so much good going on in this small church! Sadly, it was all hidden beneath the discouragement that resulted by asking the common, normal questions about their small groups.

So I asked a different set of questions oriented around MissioRelate. I discovered that group members were actually sharing life together; they were counting the cost of being in relationships that mattered; they were investing in people who did not know Jesus and helping them find the cross and then Lordship; they were involved in their communities, shared their lives with the poor; and they practiced simplicity and mutual sharing. When I entered with MissioRelate questions, I found small seeds of something awesome, yet the church and groups were not seeing the explosive growth promised in all the small group literature.

This church is practicing an alternative way of being the church, a way that stands in stark contrast from our culture and from the "easy believism" found in many churches in their area that are experiencing numeric growth. What they've developed over the last ten years is beautiful, but it does not fit conventional expectations. They are a mustard seed movement of something different, a remnant that is now asking far more powerful questions and is forming a grass roots movement of group life that moves beyond small group structures and numbers.

I've identified 21 different practices[4] that groups can do to promote mission. I break these practices into three basic rhythms, which I call Missional Communion, Missional Relating, and Missional Engagement.[5]

In the book, *The Tangible Kingdom*, the authors write of rhythms of communion, rhythms of community, and rhythms of mission. The use of such language implies that rhythms of communion and community are meant for the life of insiders and the rhythms of mission are the things that the insiders do for outsiders. In my experience, I have found that such a distinction does not match reality. Some of the most missional things that we do as groups are praying together and sharing food with one another. The way we relate to God and one another is not simply insider ministry. It is indeed missional. Consider Jesus' prayer, paraphrased by Eugene Peterson from *The Message:*

> The goal is for all of them to become one heart and mind—
> Just as you, Father, are in me, and I in you,
> So they might be one heart and mind with us.
> Then the world might believe that you, in fact, sent me.
> The same glory you gave me, I give them,
> So they'll be as unified and together as we are—
> I in them and you in me.
> Then they'll be mature in this oneness,
> And give the godless world evidence
> That you've sent me and loved them
> In the same way you've loved me. (John 17:18-23)

Reflecting on all of the chapters found in *The Tangible Kingdom*, I see plenty of evidence where, if challenged, the authors would concur with my conclusion. They tell stories of how unity and devotion to God has had an impact upon outsiders. I also don't think that the authors would say that their experience draws such a hard and fast line either.

Even if these authors don't purposely draw a dividing line between insider and outsider ministry, we as readers have been shaped in the church to think this way so we draw the line for them. We compartmentalize our church programs around such distinctions: Hospitality is a ministry to build community; prayer is for the purpose of building up the body; and serving the poor is a missions project.

Reality is far messier than our categories. To be *on mission* means that we enter into our communities with our whole lives before God, not just the part we take with us when we want to evangelize. In addition, when we engage our neighborhoods and share Jesus' life with those who don't follow him, the communication is never one sided. Those of us inside the church don't have all the answers for those outside of it. Instead, when we go *on mission* we sit and have conversations with those the church has traditionally deemed outsiders to include them in life so they can taste and see that the Lord is good.

Here are some MissioRelate questions to help guide those who are working with groups:

Missional Communion

- To what degree are our groups experiencing God's presence when they gather?
- What specific actions are individuals taking to simplify their lives so that they have time to share in community life with others?
- What kinds of sacrifices are people making to be shaped by God for leadership?
- How are people who are not Jesus followers experiencing the presence of God through the group?

Missional Relating

- How are groups working through conflict and difficult relational situations?
- How frequently are people within groups sharing meals together outside of official meetings?
- How are group members sacrificing their personal priorities for the sake of other people in the group?
- How are people who are not Jesus followers experiencing the relationships that are distinct from the world through the group?

Missional Engagement

- How are groups being led to minister outside of predetermined expectations and meet needs spontaneously?

79

- How are people using their money in unique ways to invest in redemption?
- How are groups and individuals investing in relationships in their neighborhoods?
- How are groups and individuals embracing the poor and seeking to bring redemption to social outcasts?
- How are people who are not Jesus followers encouraged to participate in the process of serving the world together?

When church leaders and groups start asking these questions, they discover they are responsible for a different set of outcomes. Instead of the typical or normal expectations about meeting attendance, group growth and other external factors, they expect to produce a life that generates a new social fabric, to use Block's terminology. The group sees itself as the context for the creation of an alternative future.

When I started asking MissioRelate questions, the old, normal questions by themselves became dissatisfying. We can still ask the old questions, but their purpose is different. For example, I now ask *numbers* questions to discover how many people are practicing the rhythms of missional community, not how many people are attending group or how many groups we currently have in operation. The questions that challenge us to live out the rhythms of missional community are the questions that empower groups to own the vision and challenge them to do life in radical ways.

Here's a difficult pill to swallow: If you want to get something different out of your groups, don't start by simply doing something different. Don't do anything at all. You will have time to learn from all the small group experts and even more time to develop new strategies. But this is not the place to begin. Begin right here, right now.

At the end of the ten chapters found in Part 2, you will find lined pages where you are invited to interact with the content of that chapter. Instead of moving on to the next chapter, take time now to reflect on what you are feeling, learning, or experiencing as you have read this chapter. What questions have shaped how you have evaluated your small groups? How do those questions influence where you invest your energy as a leader? What would it look like to change the questions that you ask? How might you begin to build that into what you do as a leader? Listen to your heart and put that on paper.

missiorelate

*An experience with others and God
that makes a difference in the world*

gather around
the presence

Ten years ago, I identified six different small group models that were producing a significant impact in North America. Four years later, I found an additional five models. Two years later, I discovered at least four more. My goal was to survey the various approaches and to determine who was actually getting it right. So I read the books, interviewed pastors, and measured results. I compared, contrasted, and looked for common structures and patterns of life.[1]

There are four primary points of distinction between all small group models, yielding four questions to understand the nuances of a specific model:

- How does the church define a group?
- How does the church support group leaders?
- What priority do groups play in the church?
- How does the church equip or disciple people within those groups?

While these questions will not cover every distinction, I have consistently found that by asking these four questions first, the answers will point to the other questions that need to be asked.

My original goal in my research was to find the *best* small group model. I wanted to tell pastors and church leaders that there was one way that was better than all the rest. I just could not find that model. There are a lot of "right" ways to do most things. My preferred small group model was no more "right" than any other. I must say that this conclusion was a bit scary. I was an ardent promoter of the cell church model. And to let go of my hold on that model sent me into a tailspin. My personal identity was wrapped up in my attachment to one model of church life.

In the midst of my own insecurity, I hungered to see what was driving the story of those who were moving beyond normalcy into a missional life. While all four of the questions are important, I found that how a group answered the first question made the biggest difference. The story that a group tells, whether normal or missional, was rooted in how the church defined the group and how the groups defined themselves.

the difference that makes all the difference: presence

Presence is the one word that can change everything. If we don't get this, we miss everything about trying to move beyond normal. Instead of trying to develop successful small groups, I am far more concerned about leading people to experience the presence of Jesus and allow that to generate a new story of mission in our midst. The presence of Jesus is central to everything.

Saint John of the Cross wrote in the sixteenth century, "Mission is putting love where love is not." How can we put love anywhere unless the one who is love is an experienced reality in our midst? Paul wrote:

> If I speak with human eloquence and angelic ecstasy but don't love, I'm nothing but the creaking of a rusty gate. If I speak God's Word with power, revealing all his mysteries and making everything plain as day, and if I have faith that says to a mountain, "Jump," and it jumps, but I don't love, I'm nothing. If I give everything I own to the poor and even go to the stake to be burned as a martyr, but I don't love, I've gotten nowhere. So, no matter what I say, what I believe, and what I do, I'm bankrupt without love.
> —1 Cor. 13:1-7 (*The Message*)

Many churches attempt to be missional without the most essential component. Love is not something we do because it is simply the right thing to do. Love is about *being*. It is the essence of who God is and it is the focus of what God wants his people to be. If we want to be on mission with God, then we must actually possess the love that he wants us to give away. And if we miss this, then all of our small groups and all of the missional stuff we do ... is "nothing."

If your goal is to develop small groups that put love where love is not, then do something that will work against everything in your ministry bones. *Slow down!* Stop looking at the mega church's small group plan out of California or New York or Illinois. Quit going to all of the blog sites that answer one how-to question after another. You can always go back to those later. What should you do instead? Get on your face before God. Call your team together and set aside the questions of strategies, goals, and budgets. Fast together. Weep together. Dream together. Change the rules. Stop what you are doing and look at what you are producing. Ask God to reveal the truth and ask,

- Where is love becoming a reality?
- Where are you experiencing more than normal?
- Who in your groups "gets it?"
- Who longs for more?
- Who hungers for a deep experience of love?
- Where is your system just a program with good strategies and good meetings?
- Where are people experiencing something good but not good enough?

We must begin with God's presence and experience his love. We cannot do MissioRelate by simply working harder at it, getting involved in evangelistic activities, doing outreach, or serving the poor. We must start with Jesus, meet with Jesus, and end with Jesus. He is the bridge builder from our normal group experience to a missional story.

87

groups without Jesus

Sadly, I am convinced that we have become so accustomed to leading groups in North America that we don't need the presence of Jesus. We know how to study the Bible and we are skilled at talking about Jesus' life and ministry. We have plenty of experience with good group discussions. Now with the advent of technology, we can pipe the best Bible teaching in the world via DVD or YouTube. We spend far more time talking about Jesus than we do encountering him. All of our energy is invested in getting our facts about the Jesus stories correct. How much energy do we invest in allowing Jesus to shape us to live out his story today?

When we experience the presence of Jesus in our groups, we shift from a mindset of studying about the stories of God, to actually embodying those stories and telling them ourselves. Our lives become an extension of God's story as the presence in our community brings the community to life.

another look at stories

The whole concept of stories can be frustrating and seemingly nebulous, yet we are shaped by stories. How we live is dependant upon how we live out our story. For instance, if a boy grows up in a home where he hears a story about hard work, earning money, and retiring wealthy, this story will shape his imagination and define success. Some who grow up with this story become driven workaholics. Others fear failure so much they attempt nothing. The actual manifestation will vary from person to person, but the narrative drives the actions or lack thereof. The key to understanding the life of a workaholic is not to dismantle workaholism, but to listen to the story he tells himself and then help him adopt a new story. Then and only then will he walk free of this unhealthy life pattern.

Every church has a story as well. This story shapes a church's life. One church has a story that is short and is based on innovation and rapid growth.

Another, possibly in the same neighborhood, has a much longer story of roots, tradition, and a rich heritage. These are the stories of the past that often go unnoticed and therefore inadvertently shape the future of the church.

Small group life is not a story about structures, types of groups, leadership training or curriculum. The small group story is primarily told by the way the people within those groups embody life together. This is the story or the narrative that is being played out in our imaginations.

Imagine a small group in your church from your past or in your current experience. When someone from outside that group looks inside, what do they see? They see a way of life, not structures or curriculum. They don't really care about how many groups a church has, what kind of books you study or how the groups are supported. They read a narrative of a kind of life being embodied within groups.

A good story is always about change. When a good story is told, one cannot walk away from it the same. I remember the first time I read *The Lion, The Witch and the Wardrobe* by C.S. Lewis. It shaped my imagination about God and it changed me.

In the same way, when we encounter Jesus in our groups, we are invited into a story of change. Any story worth reading involves change. If the characters that open a story remain the same through to the end of that same story, then why engage the story? Such static stories fill bookshelves and we don't need to waste energy by reading them. On the other hand, the classic story of Abraham is one that overwhelms with the kind of deep change required to make a good story. Abram leaves his father's family and all he knows to follow God's call. He embarks on a journey toward a home that he never actually inhabits. He is promised a son. At first, he thinks this son will be a servant. Then he assumes the promise of the son will come through Ishmael, born of a concubine. Then he has a son by his wife of 90 years of age. Finally, God calls him to sacrifice this promised son. This journey shattered Abram's world. He was invited to change on so many levels that we could read the story over and over and find new ways that this story comes to life. And when we do this, we mysteriously participate in this story and we experience change. Now that's a good story!

Encountering Jesus generates a story of hope, possibility, and change. Change is ultimately a call of repentance. I hesitate to use the word "repentance" because it is so encumbered by long use in multiple traditions of the church. In the tradition of my childhood, it was a word used to refer to what occurs at the end of a preaching service of a Billy Graham rally or while singing every verse of "Just As I Am." However, I cannot escape the fact that it is a word that shaped the imagination of God's people in the Bible. For instance, Jesus taps into the long used imagination around this word in Luke 11:

> As the crowds increased, Jesus said, "This is a wicked generation. It asks for a sign, but none will be given it except the sign of Jonah. For as Jonah was a sign to the Ninevites, so also will the Son of Man be to this generation. The Queen of the South will rise at the judgment with the people of this generation and condemn them, for she came from the ends of the earth to listen to Solomon's wisdom; and now one greater than Solomon is here. The people of Nineveh will stand up at the judgment with this generation and condemn it, for they repented at the preaching of Jonah; and now one greater than Jonah is here. – Luke 11:29-32

Jesus' use of "repent" is not related to some kind of call to "salvation" at the end of a church service. Nor is it related to "confessing our sins" because we are exhausted with our lifestyle or our moral struggles. In this passage, Jesus is calling people to shift their thinking about what God is doing in this world and realign their lives based upon it.

Jesus uses two stories to give people a different imagination about what God is doing. The story about the Queen of Sheba and the story of Jonah were both familiar to his audience. They would have quickly heard Jesus' challenge them to change the way they were responding to his ministry and the call to align themselves with him. This change was not mere emotional remorse or a matter of mental ascent. Jesus knew repentance was about life change and stories are the best way to bring about change.

In most situations, our current small group experiences (stories) have not taken us deep enough to experience this kind of change. We might do things differently—and people might even like what we are doing—but the results are normal. For example, churches have moved their Sunday school classes into home-based small groups with hopes of radical transformation. But the resulting experience is little more than the same Sunday school experience in a different location.

embracing God's presence

First, keep in mind that teaching on the importance of God's presence alone will not produce initial widespread transformation. The most you can expect from the teaching is that a few innovators will latch on to the principle and try it out. The rest might fully agree, but they will not have a clue what to do so they will do nothing. Most need to live out a new experience or experiment with it before they can personally implement it. But when those who are wired for experimentation experience the presence of Jesus in their groups, others will follow suit if they relate to these innovators as close friends.

Next, recognize that in most church settings, there are normal groups filled with people who are not ready to shape their life around the presence of Jesus. At this point in their journey, they need the normal group experience. The DVD curriculum and the Bible studies about the life and words of Jesus meet them where they are. Resist the urge to rush your normal groups into a radical new experience. It is far more productive to work with a small number of groups or even one group, helping them encounter Jesus on a regular basis. When you have experience helping one group learn a new story and experience a new rhythm, you can help additional groups.

The principle of two or three

Jesus said, "Where two or three come together in my name, there I am with them" (Matthew 18:20). In *The Relational Way*, I wrote:

91

Meeting in Christ's presence is connected to the numbers two or three. To be a church, it requires more than one person to meet in the name of Jesus. While I am not discounting the importance of private encounters in the presence of God, the Bible seems to place a much greater emphasis on the gathered people of God who meet in his presence. To cite one example, Paul writes, "But if an unbeliever or someone who does not understand comes in while everybody is prophesying, he will be convinced by all that he is a sinner and will be judged by all, and the secrets of his heart will be laid bare. So he will fall down and worship God, exclaiming, 'God is really among you!'" (1 Corinthians 14:24-25). Christ is revealed by the church, through the community of believers, not just through the words or actions of individuals. When group leaders grasp the importance of Christ's presence, they often encounter a new struggle. Too many times, groups have more than one person present, but only one person meeting in the name of Jesus: the group leader.

Everyone else is meeting in names such as, "frustration with my spouse," "fear my child will mess up his life," "exhaustion from a full day at work," or other preoccupations. While these feelings are valid and should never be ignored for the sake of a meeting, it often requires ninety minutes for the group leader to get one or two group members meeting in the name of Jesus; by that time everyone is ready to go home. It is not necessary for the entire group to meet in Jesus' name, but it is crucial that at least two or three volitionally meet in his name. Without this, most likely the group will miss the presence of Christ.

This is the reason that every group should be built around a core of two or three who are committed to meeting in the name of Jesus. Two or three can point to the center, which is Jesus. An individual who leads a group by himself can only point to himself. Jesus sent out the disciples in pairs. Paul did not go on his missionary journeys alone. Even Jesus sought companions or partners in ministry.

Small groups work best when the leader first invites two or three people to join him or her in a vision. This team then establishes the vision of meeting in Jesus' name and invites others to participate in that vision.[2]

When we think about mobilizing leaders, our tendency is to spread out our leaders as far and wide as possible so that we can minister to as many as possible. If you want to get different results, then you will need to think differently. Leaders work far better and more productively together. Instead of forming groups around one leader, consider forming groups around teams of leaders who are committed to this vision and let them discover how this works together.

While this approach might be slower, we must abandon our primary interest in growing the number of groups just to get people involved. We want to facilitate a way of life or a new story. Such a story cannot be written with only one leader. It takes a core group to live it and lead it effectively.

Michael Mack has written a very practical guide for group leaders around the principle of two or three entitled *The Pocket Guide to Burnout-Free Small Group Leadership*. In this smallish yet powerful book he writes:

Jesus had relationships with the Twelve, but he had very close, personal relationships with his inner circle of Peter, James, and John. He spent more time with them and intentionally invested into their lives. And while the Gospels do not explicitly state it, I've noticed that Jesus shared an increasing amount of leadership with these three over time. Perhaps that's why Peter was so outspoken and why James and John (or at least their mother) thought they deserved special seats next to Jesus in heaven. Note that the names of Peter, James, John, and Andrew are always mentioned first in the listing of the apostles. Why do you rarely hear anything about Bartholomew,

James son of Alphaeus, and Judas son of James? Perhaps it is because they were not the main focus of Jesus' attention. Also, the fact that Peter and John were key leaders in the early church, especially in Acts 1-6, demonstrates that they had already assumed some shared leadership in the group before Jesus' death and resurrection. (Besides the listing of the apostles in Acts 1:13, the apostle James' name is mysteriously missing in the rest of Acts. But we know he was still active; he was the first of the apostles to be martyred—Acts 12:2.)

Why did Jesus choose three men as his inner circle? Three is a significant number in Scripture. The Godhead consists of three persons. Noah had three sons, who repopulated the earth after the flood. Abraham met with three visitors (probably Christ and two angels). Jesus was in the tomb three days. The Holy City that comes down out of heaven will have three gates on every side. I'm amazed by how often Scripture refers specifically to two or three:

- "Two are better than one [but] a cord of three strands is not quickly broken" (Ecclesiastes 4:9-12).
- "Do not entertain an accusation against an elder unless it is brought by two or three witnesses" (1 Timothy 5:19; also see Deuteronomy 17:6; 19:15; Matthew 18:16; 2 Corinthians 13:1; and Hebrews 10:28).
- "Where two or three come together in my name, there am I with them" (Matthew 18:20).
- "Two or three prophets should speak, and the others should weigh carefully what is said" (1 Corinthians 14:29).

I'm not saying there is anything "magical" about a core group of three. I want to be clear that I'm not advocating a new program or system for small groups consisting of no more than three or four people. I'm simply pointing out that there are limits to the total number of people you can effectively lead, shepherd, and disciple. And I believe that number is two or three.[3]

A few years ago, I met with two pastors who had developed an extensive small group system. When mentioned the idea of leading groups as teams, their immediate response was, "That sure will slow things down for us. We would need *twice* the number of leaders." They were correct. If our goal is the presence of Jesus, then slower may be the wise choice.

Before you move on to the next chapter, I want you to stop and think about your immediate reaction to this chapter. Then begin to think about some of the people who "get it" in your church. Who are your best leaders who love God, love people and have a deep desire to share God's love with people who don't have it? Write their names on the following personal reflection pages. Spend some time praying for each of them. Reflect on how they do leadership. Do they have a team, or are they spread out thinly operating alone? What is the state of their soul? Have you had a conversation with them about that lately? What do you sense God saying to you about these people? Write down what you sense God saying.

missiorelate
*An experience with others and God
that makes a difference in the world*

focus on
kingdom formation

Great stories depend upon great characters. It's not enough to have a strong plot and riveting action. Characters with deep impact drive the stories that affect us and are remembered. Some of the most dynamic stories ever written are found within the 66 books of the Bible. They are full of intrigue, action, success and failure, and life and death situations. You don't have to look hard to find transforming characters such as Noah, Abraham, Joseph, Samuel, David, Jesus, and Paul. God's grand story is described with regular people who are being formed for life in his kingdom.

In chapter 3, I referenced the story of Abraham and how YHWH asked him to leave behind his family and his land to embark upon a journey that re-formed his identity. One of the ways the Bible points to this forming process was through the changing of one's name. As he followed YHWH, his name was changed from Abram to Abraham. God didn't improve Abraham, he transformed him.

When we look to move from normal groups to missional groups, there must be a greater goal than improvement. To generate a new story, we must focus on the formation of people . . . characters who will live out the story of mission. Another word for this is discipleship. We are not in the business of creating groups, or even missional small groups. We are in the business of discipling people and small groups are a great way to organize and facilitate that business.

discipled by normal

Much of how we have launched groups and then promoted them has been based around meeting the needs of individuals. In a way, the small group movement has fallen prey to *syncretism*, a term used by missionaries to describe a watered-down form of the gospel compromised by the beliefs and practices of a culture.

Instead of confronting individualism and self-actualization, normal small groups have been conditioned by non-missional values and they reinforce a normal life. This leads me to a crucial question. How do we shape groups for missional life unless we directly challenge the cultural systems that have shaped the life of the "successful" American church? Think about it: as we look across the landscape of what a successful church looks like, we assume that numbers is the key. One of the pastors I follow on Twitter recently commented, "If a church is not growing, 99% of the reasons for it are internal." What if he's dead wrong? What if the reason behind a church's growth is the individualistic message preached and the church's groups that fit nicely into the American dream? Growth in the American small group movement has been—by enlarge—a result of a syncretistic message: "We can have all that this world has to offer and be a Christian too! Let's get together and talk about it." This is punctuated by the formation and expansion of small groups that study what they want, meet as little as they need to, and live the way they want without sacrifice.

You may be thinking, "What if a church loses people because the leadership challenges people to serve the poor, and not just serve them but to get to know them? What if the leadership challenges the sin of racism and then does something about it, like hiring a person of color to join their staff? And what if the leadership moves beyond having nice small group meetings to helping people start living a life of simplicity? Are those things that will grow a church?" Maybe not.

To move beyond the normal group life that comes with syncretistic thinking, we need to think theologically about the call to participate in the kingdom of God, which is the reign of God, the rule of God, or where people operate according to the order of the King. The hope set before us in MissioRelate is the kingdom of God, the realized order of God's life and ways in our midst. In order to move into God's ways and move out of the ways of the world that have crept into the church, we must cast a vision for the kingdom and nothing less. A vision for small groups, personal growth, or even the experience of community falls far short of the radical vision for the kingdom of God.

the root of the problem

Small groups in North America have been developed out of an a-theological imagination. Now before you assume that I am judging you or your small group model, continue reading with an open mind and heart. I admit that most who start small groups share common theological reasons for doing so. We say that small groups were used in the New Testament and therefore we should use them today. Or, we tap into the social Trinity model and we conclude that since God the Father, Son and Spirit are community, we must do life in community. Beyond these points, there is little theology that shapes what we do, and that's where small group ministry has gone awry. When we take on the job of small group champion or participate on a team to oversee group life, we don't think about the extended theology under which we should operate. We ask pragmatic questions about how to do small groups to get more people involved. Small group pastors are held accountable for their numbers and growth, not for their theology or their biblical imagination, so the numbers and growth become the main focus and sometimes, the sole focus.

Argue with me if you like, but the only aspect of church life that requires any theological training is providing the weekly sermon. Everything else about church life falls under the imagination of church organization or administration. For example, a person need not have a theological imagination to oversee

children's ministry. He or she only needs the ability to recruit, train, and organize people for the program and a heart for children. Small group pastors are
no different. They are required to operate according to this administrative
imagination with a priority to get people in groups and improve group life.
It's all about pacifying the needs of the organization.

If this is true—and I believe it is—syncretism is almost impossible to
avoid. To avoid the dilution of the gospel in groups in creating normal groups,
we must think theologically about how people live, not just how people do
group meetings. People will faithfully attend a weekly group meeting; they
will even be some of the best leaders in the church and still live a syncretistic
life. We must begin to think theologically about life patterns and not just
think about what our group systems may or may not be producing.

If you found out that one of your small group leaders is struggling with
a moral sin (getting drunk and being abusive toward his family) you know
what to do. Everyone understands that we need to deal with moral issues like
this directly and immediately. But what about the sin of being inhospitable to
one's neighbors? Now we're in territory we've never cared about, or not cared
about nearly as much as the leader struggling with alcohol and abuse.

Churches require their most mature leaders to participate in so many
activities at the church building that they don't have much time to be hospitable toward their neighbors. They are too busy and overly consumed with
church stuff to even consider that there is a need on their street that Jesus
wants to meet. Preparing a meal and inviting a neighbor over for conversation
is an overwhelming thought with all they do for the church. Missional stories
are generated when we reflect theologically on how we do life and make room
to live outside the norms of our church subculture.

Theology vs. individualism

In his book, *The Search to Belong*, Joseph Myers proposes that about 33% of any
given congregation desires to participate in a small group. From this statistic,
he argues that a church should not try to force people into small group life
but allow them to relationally remain where they are. On one hand, he raises a

good point. Community cannot be forced upon those who don't want it or see a current need for it. Leading people in this way is unnatural. If our culture is shaped by individualism, this data and Myers' conclusion are not surprising. Why would people desire something that does not fit the way they do life?

Actually, I think that Myers observation points us in a different direction. Instead of backing off of the experience of community, we should be asking questions about our missional situation so that we understand why our culture has so much trouble living in community. If we think theologically, then we cannot tolerate or support syncretism built on individualism. To do this, we must carefully examine our local context. If you were being trained as a missionary to go to a place like Southeast Asia, you would learn about the culture and the inherent theology of that culture. You would not assume that all the parts of that culture line up with the gospel.

What keeps our groups normal? Rampant individualism characterized by long commutes alone in cars; making big life decisions in isolation; working far too many hours each week; spending huge sums of money on personal items; moving residences every three to five years; and changing churches even more frequently to suit personal or family needs. We need to first develop a theological imagination to understand how individualism shapes our culture and our church life and then develop discipleship practices that counteract it.

Theology vs. suburban life

I am a staff pastor in what is classified as a mega-church. About two years before my family moved here, I was invited to lead a training seminar. To my shock and surprise, I did not find what I expected. Instead of driving through a suburban neighborhood, the route to the church building was through a rather dated, under-resourced area of Saint Paul. The building was (and still is) unimpressive. The church purchased a closed Builder's Square warehouse and remodeled it and the signage goes unnoticed for the most part.

I did not notice the significance of this to our small groups at first. Our church includes people from all kinds of socioeconomic backgrounds, from suburbanites to those who are mired in generational poverty. As I analyzed the group data, I found we were able to build groups comprised of people with a middle class background, even if they lived in the inner city. But most of those who were under-resourced or from marginalized cultures were not involved in a small group.

Around the world, small groups pervade church life in ways that we can only imagine in North America. In large part, the international small group movement is an urban-based phenomenon. But this is not the case in North America. Review the primary small groups books that highlight America and you'll find that almost every example is a suburban church. They are located in towns or cities where there is strong, new population growth or the area has experienced new growth over the last 20 years. Historically, small group growth follows a suburban sprawl.

Have we crossed the boundary from being culturally relevant to actually bowing down to the culture? When I wrestle with the Bible's constant reference to ministering to and taking up the plight of the under-resourced, I've concluded that normal groups practice syncretism. If all we are doing is connecting to people who are just like us and have the same problems and victories as we do, then are we stuck in normal and missing out on the kind of community that fits the kingdom?

Again, this requires that you and I think theologically about our contexts. The physical location of the building where my church meets on the weekends forces us to ask these questions. But just because a church building is located in a middle class suburban location, does that mean that it is only called to facilitate community for that segment of society? I've found that those who are financially stable learn more from the under-resourced than the other way around. Suburban churches need the people of the city.

Once we begin to think in this new way, it will impact the kinds of small group structures that we develop. Instead of duplicating what works elsewhere, we turn our attention to our contexts and what small groups should look like within those contexts. The structures we develop will vary from place to place. Being missional in Seattle is vastly different and calls for a radically different imagination than being missional in Dallas. To go even further with this line of thought, a small group that is comprised of middle-class suburanites will look vastly different than one made up of under-resourced people in the city. The latter might not even meet in homes, but at some kind of neutral site. To think theologically about our context means that we have to do away with the one-way-fits all mentality.

Ultimately, the key is not about groups and what kinds of groups work at all. The key is think about discipleship and what God wants to form in us in all kinds of contexts, suburban, urban, various ethnic groups, etc.

Theology vs. "goods and services" groups

Normal groups are designed to meet people where they are, providing spiritual goods and services for individuals who are looking for a group to help them become a better Christian. If the purpose of the church is to provide programs—including small groups that keep people engaged and content—then normal groups are a good fit. But should we be asking if we are being syncretistic, allowing the broader culture to dictate the church's purpose? Absolutely.

If we desire to lead our groups beyond the normal experience, we must do much more than creating groups that meet spiritual needs. We must create environments where people have the opportunity to confront these assumptions of our culture about what church is. Being missional is a way of life, not a task we perform outside the walls of our church buildings to get people to join us inside. Being missional is engaging our culture with the gospel. If most of the people who now populate our churches have been shaped by the practices of the wider culture, then part of our immediate mission is to re-shape our life together as a church. The way we live together is the way we do mission. The way we imagine the church will impact that mission. We cannot conclude that mission is just about helping the poor or opening a coffee shop. It must begin by creating a pattern of doing life together that stands in contrast to the practices of the wider culture.

This is what discipleship is about. If we want to move beyond giving people what they want so that they will attend groups, we must intentionally help them reshape "what they want" so that their wants begin to line up with the wants of the kingdom.

discipled for mission

Recently it hit me that some of the churches that have developed outstanding small group systems are not based upon small groups at all. They are actually doing small groups for the sake of discipleship. Their goal is not small group participation. Instead, it's helping small groups of people confront the typical American life. These churches are aiming to generate an alternative way of life. Small groups for the sake of small groups will always be blown by the wind of the culture. But small groups for the sake of discipleship have a deeper, trans-formational, and missional purpose.

Elizabeth O'Connor writes of the missional experience of The Church of the Savior in Washington D.C. She states, "This deepening of the spiritual life is not spontaneous. People do not just become great Christians. They grow as they make certain purposeful responses to life and to the grace of God. We call these ordered responses 'disciplines.'"[1]

In the monastic tradition, these ordered responses were shaped by what they call a "rule." Hence, Saint Benedict created a rule of life for all those who chose to enter into a Benedictine community. While I am not advocating a certain monastic tradition for small groups, we should learn from Benedict's specificity. We need to develop a "rule," or what I call *rhythms*. These rhythms identify specific patterns for living as God's people during this time, therefore causing us to stand in contrast to the surrounding culture. O'Connor again helps us see the importance of this:

> As members of a mission group we need to be disciplined and we need to be willing to require a discipline of those who would be on mission with us. No person or group or movement has vigor and power unless it is disciplined. Are we willing to be disciplined ourselves and to require it of others when it means that we will be the

target of the hostilities and the pressures of many who do not see the necessity? The chances are that we will give in unless we know that this "giving in" means that our mission group will have not hard sharp cutting edge and will in time peter out.[2]

Few would be so blunt today. This book was written in 1963. One might discount the writings due to its age. However, it is based on timeless wisdom. She continues with:

This does not mean that we exclude a person from the Christian community. It simply means that we define his [or her] participation in the mission. We do not ask him to articulate what he does not know, or subject him to pressures for which he is not ready. The army does not take a man, put a gun in his hand, and march him to the front when he has never held a gun and does not know how to load it.[3]

In their book, *Organic Disciplemaking*, Dennis McCallum and Jessica Lowery write about how their church has been built upon the truths that O'Connor wrote about 50 years ago:

Xenos is a local church that grew up spontaneously beginning in 1970, during the Jesus Movement. ... Leaders are not recognized unless they are truly making disciples. With over 250 student and adult home churches, each led by a team of three to six leaders, the church has over 500 recognized leaders and around 900 "servant team" members. All servant team members must show they are working with disciples before being accepted to the team. Throughout the church, most people are either being discipled or are discipling others.[4]

Another example is Antioch Church in Waco, Texas. Their small groups are not just places for people to get connected and study the Bible. They have set an expectation that people will be shaped to live radical, sacrificial lives and that is the genuine "normal Christian life." The founding leader, Jimmy Seibert, writes, "Discipleship was the foundation for everything we had started in 1987 and continues to be a major part of everything we do today."[5]

If we want MissioRelate in our small groups, the first question we need to ask is *not* "What kind of small group can be missional?" or "What can we do to be missional?" Instead we must ask, "How are we going to create a culture of discipleship that will form people for mission? Prepare yourself for a shift in mindset regarding discipleship. You'll need it to birth MissioRelate groups.

I grew up in a church based on the assumption that discipleship was something that was the responsibility of the individual. For this reason, when I started working with churches to help them form small groups, I did not connect the priority of discipleship with the experience of missional community. Ralph Neighbour invested much of his energy on developing group systems, but he spent even more of his time creating patterns that will help grow disciples though life-on-life interaction. For ten years, I worked for the ministry he created to promote this relational discipleship pattern, but I never really understood the importance of it during my time there. My focus was on small groups. We talked about discipleship in our training, but that seemed to take a back seat to groups. But in Ralph's original thinking, it was clearly the other way around. Today, I see that discipleship is not the responsibility of the individual, but of the leaders in the church. A movement of discipleship begins as leaders start mentoring and investing in a small number of people.

For example, Neil Cole writes about Life Transformation Groups, which he uses to form people within the organic churches that he oversees. A group of three meets together weekly for the sake of personal conversations about their life and their walk in Christ. It can grow to four but no bigger. And once it does grow to four, the members of the group look to include two others and create two groups of three.[6]

John Wesley understood the importance of these discipling relationships more than anyone. He called them bands, which were sub-groupings of his small groups. In the bands, they would deal with questions about how they lived their lives, challenging one another to move away from a life shaped by the larger culture and embrace love.[7]

The work of Greg Ogden has proven to be very helpful in this front for my friend Jim Egli. In his work as a small groups pastor, the leadership of the church has helped group members connect in groups of four. They meet for six to nine months together, working through Ogden's book *Discipleship Essentials*. Afterwards, they encourage each person to connect with three others and repeat the process. Jim told me that this has brought life transformation to his groups more than anything else the church has tried through the years.[8]

Establishing people to live out the kingdom by abandoning individualism and embracing discipleship as a core value will not be a fast process for the church filled with normal groups. But I don't believe God is in a hurry like many of us.

Invest a few minutes right now and use the next page to reflect on a couple of important matters. First, as you read through the sections where I wrote about how we think theologically about small groups, what was your immediate, knee-jerk response? Recall this and stop to see what God might be saying to you. Second, think about the current role discipleship plays in your church if it has a role at all. How is it related to small groups and the experience of community? What could be different?

missiorelate
An experience with others and God
that makes a difference in the world

leverage
reality

I n 1999, I received a phone call from Karen Hurston. Her father, John Hurston, was the missionary who mentored David Yongii Cho, the pastor of the church in South Korea that grew to over 275,000 members by meeting in small groups. Cho has been credited as the innovator of small home groups and Karen Hurston grew up in his church. As an adult, she became a consultant helping churches develop small group systems.

In our conversation, she shared this observation: "In the 1970s, there was a wave of interest in small groups. Then it waned. In the 1980s, another wave of interest arose and the same was true of the 1990s. But we have yet to see group life that is bringing about radical transformation." She then asked, "How can we learn from these experiences so that we are not just reproducing the same results with each wave?"

I am a dreamer. I love to sit and talk about biblical ideas and strategic plans that seem impossible to implementers and managers. My fellow team members at the church tell me that I think about ideas that we can implement two years from now, not this semester or quarter. It is true that I have difficulty thinking about what I need to get done today because I am dreaming about things we can do down the road. And most of my dreams and visions are based around how we can facilitate and create communities that are on mission. But having dreams and visions for community and mission is not enough. Having great ideas about how mission fosters community does not actually pan out in reality. During that phone conversation years ago, Karen was expressing her concern about wave after wave of visionary dreamers who talked about missional community, but the vision never came to fruition. How do we deal with this reality so that we can lead people from their current experience into a new story?

why visions and dreams
fail to take us into missiorelate

As I shared earlier, I worked with Ralph Neighbour and his team for 10 years as a writer, researcher, and consultant. Ralph was the person who introduced the American church to the concept of the cell church model, providing practical instructions on how to set up a church structure like the one that led to the radical growth in churches like Yoido Full Gospel Church in South Korea, Elim Church in El Salvador (now 180,000 members) Dion's Robert's church in the Ivory Coast (now with over 200,000 members) and other churches like this. This strategy is characterized by small groups of people who gathered weekly and shared life together with the intention to encourage one another and reach out to non-Christians and include them in the life of the group. Doing this resulted in group growth and multiplication.

In the 1990s, we could not keep up with all the churches coming to us to find out how to implement this strategy. The vision we had was compelling and hopeful. However, in communicating the dreams for the church and the strategies that supported our dreams, I observed all four stories at work. While I know that I have highlighted how the four stories have played out in previous chapters, the following reports the four stories from four different churches that tried to implement the same model of small group life. The reason I use this model is that historically, at its roots, it has one of the most radical and inspiring visions of all that have been promoted over the last 20 years.

The story of a cell church improvement *strategy*

Second Church is a successful church located in a mid-size city in the south. Its senior pastor was one of the best and brightest leaders in the region. Traditionally, this church had grown through Sunday School, which required building more and more physical space for classrooms. After the last addition, they filled up all of their new Sunday school classrooms the first week. What were they to do? This church came to us to find a new way to connect people so that they did not have to build more buildings. From us they found a way to improve their already good church experience.

Second Church learned how to prioritize group life, set up the structures, and do the training. They were able to get 80% of their 2000 people into groups. They explained how groups would improve their lives and the church and it did just that. People loved small groups and it was exciting right up to the day they hit a brick wall. It did not provide the improvement they desired. So Second Church went looking for new strategies. They created all kinds of groups that people would join because they were based on interest or self-improvement. Cooking groups, biking groups, and quilting groups popped up overnight. Anything that would get people connected by tapping into what people already wanted is what Second Church created. This church focused so much on the strategy of group involvement that they failed to assess what this strategy was producing. As a result, they just developed a new structure to gather people in the same way of life that they had before.

The story of a cell church adjustment *strategy*

The leadership of a church of 150 attended a large cell church conference. They were sold on the idea as a way to grow their church and impact the people in their very large city. They attended our training, bought our resources, and even invited Ralph Neighbour to personally train their leaders. Groups were established because the pastor asked the people to make group life a priority and they obeyed.

The church even prioritized the groups by modifying the weekly schedule of church life. They closed the mid-week service so groups could meet during the week and changed the Sunday night service to a weekly training time for group leaders. They adjusted everything about the church calendar and asked people to adjust their lives accordingly. Small groups became *the* primary tool for growing the church and helping people connect. This is exactly the practical steps that we taught people to take and they followed our recommendations to a tee.

But the resulting story was rather banal. The groups weren't bad, but they weren't anything to write about either. They were traditional groups that the leadership pronounced to be the center of the church's life. The problem is that these groups did not deserve such a lofty label. As a result, the leaders went searching for other strategies, started tweaking how the groups were organized, reworked how they wrote the weekly curriculum, and de-emphasized the importance of the groups. The underlying assumption was, "If we change the plan, we will change outcome."

The story of a cell church revision *strategy*

The Hills Church in Northern California was a small traditional church that recently took on a new name. The pastor came to us recognizing that they had no potential to grow, little money to maintain what they had, and they possessed no passion to engage the people in the culture. The leadership learned the same principles, language and structures as the previous two churches, but the difference was that this church understood the need to revise its culture and church rhythms to fit the new structure. They began by asking hard questions about their expectations of people and how they participated in the life of the church. They realized how they could use their weekly Sunday services as a launching point for something new, and then they transformed what was a very good Sunday evening service into an equipping time so that people would understand what it meant for them to participate in group life.

Next, they helped people process the expectations of being committed to participate in the life of the church community. They did far more than get people into groups. They established what they called The Community Practice, which included practical ways that they were going to live in community, including statements such as:

- We will center our time together around the presence of Jesus.
- We will work through conflict even when we want to run away.
- We will make room in our lives for each other so that we spend time together outside the meeting.
- We will speak honestly to one another.
- We will open our lives and not keep secrets from one another.

This church was less worried about assimilating a high percentage of their people into groups and more concerned about establishing a way of life together that is distinctively Christian. They realized that this might seem radical and the groups would not grow as quickly. From this experience has come a group of people who understand what it means to live in such a way that they actually love one another in distinctively "Jesus" ways.

The story of a cell church re-creation *strategy*

While cell church strategies were the rave in the mid 1990s, they have lost their appeal today. Those who thought the magic was in the strategy have moved on, but there are a few who understood that there was something beyond. They made a lot of mistakes along the way, but they have figured out how they can live out the story of re-creation in their context. One example of this is a church in a Southwestern state, which was originally a part of an established traditional church. The college minister developed his branch of the church around the cell church strategy. He took his time and did not expect to restructure the entire church around this strategy. Instead, he invested in leaders, challenged them to count the cost of discipleship, established accountability structures within groups, and developed a leadership training process. They were doing much more than developing groups. They were inviting people to enter a journey of learning what it means to be on mission.

Eventually, this college ministry grew and was birthed out to plant a new church. They did not set out to start a new church. They simply worked with the people they had and developed a way of life and then discerned God's leading in the midst. Today, they have a school of discipleship where they challenge young people to take a year off work or school and go through an intense training and get exposure to churches in foreign countries. The "normal" in their groups is to live in missional community in abnormal ways.

the reality of the stories

All four of these churches had the same vision and they were trained with the same strategies. And while there are many differences between these churches, I found a difference that had a huge impact: the leaders in the last two stories dealt with the realities that their people faced and led them into the vision, while the leaders in the first two stories focused only on their vision and strategy for small group community.

I remain convicted about this very thing in my own ministry, which is the need to lead the people in my church from a perspective of reality. I blogged about it recently and wrote this:

30 miles north of Dallas, you will find hundreds of acres once owned by my grandparents, who operated a dairy farm. My grandfather sold the property in the 1960s. When I was a kid, my father rented the land from the new owner for raising beef cattle. We also raised sheep, chickens, and even rabbits at one point of my childhood. We cultivated wheat, oats, and hay as well. Through my veins runs the dirt, sweat, and tears of generations of farmers.

I learned a lot on the farm. For one, I learned that it is hard work. While I'm not medically allergic to farm labor it sure felt like it. But there is another lesson that shaped my imagination, one that applies to my work now as a pastor. I learned from my father that caring for animals begins by working with what you have, not what you *wish* you had.

What exactly does this mean, to work with what you have not what you wish you had? If you grew up on a farm, you know exactly what this means. Farmers have no time whatsoever to spend dreaming about what they wish they had. They specialize in dealing with reality. Even if they want to grow their farm to be different, they spend their time and effort working within their current reality to get it there. This is true whether one is working with animals or crops.

My father rented some land to raise hay for horses. In the first two or three years, we did not expect that land to produce good hay. Our first crops were used to feed cows, which can eat low quality hay in a way that horses cannot. After a year a two, we were able to cultivate hay of higher quality that we could sell to horse ranchers.

I think that pastoral leaders could learn a few things from farmers like my father. There is a tendency within church leadership circles to think about the church not in terms of reality, but in terms of what they *wish* the church was like. We assume the people we lead are in one place, when in reality their lives and the issues they face put them in quite a different place. So we develop visions, make plans, and implement strategies. With good intentions, we live in a dream world about what the church might look like. The church we dream about is of certain legitimate size, has an acceptable place to meet, and has an organization that keeps it running smoothly. To make this dream work, we try to fit people into our plans to live it out and make it a reality. Again, with good intentions and usually out of much prayer and devotion we develop these plans. But I do think we fail to actually meet people in their current reality. We assume that they are in a more spiritual and better place than they really are with the idea we can leverage this maturity to realize our dream of the ideal church.

Let me illustrate. When we think about starting small groups, pastors have often set goals for small group growth. Years ago, I remember a pastor putting a sign up in his worship center that read "2000 groups by 2000." He thought that would be motivating. Another pastor promoted a vision in his home country of Singapore of a small group on every floor of every apartment building. Now the rave is to promote a certain percentage of group participation. I know of churches that brag about 80% or 100% participation in small groups. Such talk is "pastor talk" not "people talk." It does not meet people where they are. This has nothing to do with the realties that people face.

What does a single mom with five kids care about how many small groups are in her church? She might not even see the need to participate in a group. Or maybe the groups she has been a part of have not dealt with the realities that she faces. How about the over-worked man who is afraid of losing his job? Or the couple who is afraid that their kids might be on drugs? Or the widow who has given in to depression? Or even the faithful leader in the church who looks at such visions and goals and thinks, "Yikes! That sounds like a lot of work."

As leaders, we are concerned about developing a church that works well. We want a church that closes the back door, does body ministry, and even grows through evangelism. These are great goals, but we need to think of them out of an awareness of the realities that people face, not out of the wish-based dreams of where we *hope* people are.

Most of the people in our culture (and a part of our churches) are shaped by the imagination of individualism and don't feel the need for relationships in the church. The way they do life is already full of so much busyness and people that the thought of joining a small group is not crucial to them and it certainly won't fit into their current lifestyle. They might want a Bible study, but they don't feel the need for biblical community that would live in such a way that would make a difference in the world.

The reality for those in the normal experience

Writing is often frustrating, especially when I think I have written something well and then my editor tells me more work is required. While writing my previous book, my editor called me to tell me that the draft he just read was too idealistic, judgmental, and quite frankly "undoable." He commented, "My small group could never do what you are talking about." In other words, it did not meet real people in real small groups where they were.

I realized that I had failed to include a significant chunk of material that I teach in my seminars. The first seminar where I taught the material was at a 150-year-old Lutheran Church in the inner city of Saint Paul. As people arrived, I estimated that about 60% of the group was over the age of 50, which was intimidating because I'm in my early 40s. In teaching seminars for 15 years, I had not been effective at helping that generation enter into group life. In the past, this group repeatedly heard the grandiose dreams of what the church could be and were not interested in my ideals. But this day was different. I shared an illustration I left out of that first draft of the book:

God's vision was to provide his people with the Promised Land. This was the hope of Moses as well. He was not interested in delivering the people out of slavery alone because he was familiar with the promises to Abraham. After all, Moses had something to do with the actual writing of the first five books of the Bible.

If we were to map the shortest route on land possible from the Egypt to the Promised Land, it would take about a month to six weeks for a group of people on-mission to travel this route. The actual route the Israelites took was anything but direct. What exactly was going on for 40 years of wilderness wandering when God's dream for his people was the Promised Land?

God was patiently dealing with their reality so that he might prepare His people to enter into his vision.

When I spoke to those 70 Lutherans about Israel's four decade journey, I saw the connection in the faces of people with many years of church experience. After our day together, a retired school principle came up to me and thanked me saying, "This is the first time someone actually dealt with our realities and didn't simply lay out a nice plan. Now I know why all of our previous small group plans never worked like we had hoped."

We must meet people in the wilderness and lead them from that point. For instance, the idea of perpetual or long-term groups actually sets most Christians up for failure. The only way to break out for many is for the group to fail. Of course, we tell them that the dream is for the group to grow and multiply, but most people in groups don't have the relational skills needed to navigate group conflict. If we start actually helping groups deal with conflict after it comes, it's too late. But I'm getting ahead of myself. I deal with this more in a later chapter.

Here's another excellent example if you've yet to catch what I'm pitching. I remember when I first became a small group leader. I assumed that it was a life-long commitment. At the very least, it was an open-ended commitment. When I planned to move to Canada to continue my studies, my pastor came to me and challenged me to stay. My departure would not help him achieve his church dream.

Reality requires us to pastor and lead people within their current situations, which includes facts such as Americans moving on average once every three and half years; we watch way too much television which gets in the way of relationship development; and we are overcommitted with our time. A compelling vision or dream for missional community will not change this. We have been shaped by the world in which we live and telling small groups to be missional will not change how we are shaped.

In my current role as a pastor, we have decided to emphasize shorter group commitments for people who are learning to do community. I believe this is the power behind six-week church-wide campaigns. Short-term small groups provide opportunities for people to put their toe in the water without having to make open-ended commitments. Then, the group can discern together their next steps. But even as groups move beyond this six-week commitment, we now must help them commit to a time period of no more than nine months. This fits within the reality that groups are not perpetual and that most people are learning to do group life.

To some, this might sound like a diluted version of a radical small group vision for group multiplication and mission. I guess in some ways it is, if you assume that these short-term kinds of groups are the end goal. But in the MissioRelate conversation, we have no desire to simply keep people in short-term experiences or some kind of semester group. We want to use these groups to expose the participants to something far greater. The idea is to help them catch a vision for more and begin to process what a different kind of community might look like. Instead of giving them visions and dreams from the top down, we are creating environments that help them discover the vision for themselves.

the reality for those who are in missiorelate

When a group moves from normal life into the story of Relational Revision, it enters into a time of formation. This is spiritual formation for mission. The group will journey together as a community and work together to do life differently. They might even journey together as a group among other groups. A few small groups might work together to be on mission in a specific way in a neighborhood.

As a group experiences more and more of Relational Revision it then moves into Missional Re-creation. This is not so much a prescribed shift, as it is a discovery along the way. When this happens, the forms of group life will vary based on the giftings of the group members and the needs of the community. For instance, when most talk about small groups, the goal is for groups to reach people and then enfold them into the larger church. I know of a small group comprised of single, under-educated moms living below the poverty line. Most likely, these women will never come to our weekend services. They just don't relate to the longer sermons and the style of the Sunday morning gathering. This group must live in re-creation and see how it can take on new forms of being God's people. To ask them to conform to the patterns of established church life will stymie the life God is creating in their midst.

This morning I spoke with a friend who is a small group coach in his church. He is clearly frustrated with the normalcy of most of his groups, so I asked him a few questions about his passion. His heart beats for his unique neighborhood and especially for a new apartment building just down the road. Now he is gathering people who live near him to begin to pray for this neighborhood, to walk the streets and get to know people, and begin to connect with people in these apartments. He wants to create small groups that fit the people in that building and let them follow God's leading to shape these groups. The shape of the groups will not be predetermined by the central leadership of his church. The leadership will only help to establish the rhythms, but how those rhythms are played will depend upon the groups themselves.

Some might read this and think, "Great! I can just create any kind of group I want." This misses the point. Imagine Jim who likes to play volleyball and hang out with others who play volleyball. Every Saturday morning a group from the church comes together to play. It is even considered one of the official groups of the church. This is a great example of the Free-market small group system,[1] often resulting in more of the same, normal small groups that are better than nothing, but fall short of God's dream. Such a group might very well fit the reality that Jim and his volleyball friends face in life, but to make that the dream or goal of a group fails to lead them into a new reality.

But there is another way a group can meet people at their point of reality and invite them into mission. A couple of members of a group are weekend mechanics. They decide to pool their resources, including combining some of their tools and selling off the extras and work together on the weekends. They meet people in their neighborhood who see them working on their cars and they engage them around how they could serve them. They even offer an oil-change day. Some other people from the neighborhood want to learn how to take care of their cars so they hold a short car-care workshop once a month.

From these actitivies, which they sensed a missional call to do together, they have been able to build relationships, fix cars for people who cannot afford the repairs, and talk about Jesus throughout the process. Because of this, various group members are sharing occasional meals with neighbors and people are becoming open about how their previous experiences of church have fallen short of what they are looking for.

In this story, people in the neighborhood are seeing the love of God in action and participate in a missional group from the beginning. In most cases, when people begin their relationship with God in a missional way, they are much more likely to enter into active discipleship. They don't get caught in the trap of thinking that the church is there to meet their needs.

Now it's your turn. On the next couple of pages, reflect on how you lead. Are you naturally a visionary leader or one who leads from where people are today? How do you need to balance both to move your people toward the kingdom? Take time and write down some of the realities that your people face outside of their church commitments. How do you need to change in order to lead people within their real contexts?

missiorelate
*An experience with others and God
that makes a difference in the world*

help people answer life questions

Whenever I interact with people about being missional, most think they have a solid understanding of the concept. After all, the church is big into missions, our members have taken short-term mission trips, and we've sent money to missionaries overseas for many years. "Missions" described with these examples defines something that a church chooses to do outside of its normal rhythms. Church is what we do in a basically Christian culture while missions is something that we do for people outside that Christian culture.

Therefore, the term missional community (or missional small groups) is often interpreted as a group of people who choose to perform a set of tasks for another group of people outside the church or outside the group. It is typically something they do for the unchurched. So some conclude that a group that cooks at a homeless shelter once a month or packs food boxes for needy families is missional in nature. Others assume that missional small groups are about evangelism, employing servanthood and relational outreach strategies.

This presents a problem. Both the missions and relational evangelism perspectives can turn *missional* into a task to be performed for those outside the group. The insiders have the right information and they go to prescribe what they have for the outsiders. For example, in groups that emphasize relationship evangelism I have found that the focus was on "getting people to come to my group" and not about what Jesus was doing in their lives. As a small group leader, I remember making "evangelism" plans for our group so that we could connect with the unchurched. Our intentions were good, but we turned the unchurched into projects because we assumed that we knew what they needed. We were trained with a set of prescribed answers. We knew what they needed, whether they wanted it or not.

Here's the truth: being missional is not about a task or work to be done that is based on the assumption that we as insiders know what the outsider needs. It is not about doing nice things for them or "getting them saved" and into our groups or congregation. They may very well participate in the life of the group in the future, but a MissioRelate group does not turn people into projects.

Challenging this perspective is very difficult for many. We naturally divide activities between those things that are for group insiders and things that are for outsiders. Worship, prayer, teaching, and fellowship are for insiders. Outsiders need what we have on the inside. In other words, the "missio" part is for outsiders and the "relate" part is for insiders as they love God and one another.

MissioRelate eliminates the walls of insider versus outsider activities. It is a way of life where what has traditionally been viewed as insider stuff—discipleship, Bible study, small group meetings, worship, spiritual disciplines, and community—are done so that others can see. That which has been viewed as outsider stuff—community service, serving the poor, praying for the needs of a community, and sharing our faith are done with others so that they see the life of the group and even participate in the relationships of the group. Most importantly, these things take place before or even without expectations that people will become a part of a small group.

Jesus said, "All authority in heaven and on earth has been given to me. Therefore go and make disciples of all nations, baptizing them in the name of the Father and of the Son and of the Holy Spirit, and teaching them to obey everything I have commanded you. And surely I am with you always, to the very end of the age."[1] The verb "go" can be translated as active, as it is in most modern English Bibles. But in the Greek it is not an active verb and it can also be translated "as you go." Eugene Peterson's paraphrase of this passage in *The Message* catches this meaning beautifully:

> Go out and train everyone you meet, far and near, in this way of life, marking them by baptism in the threefold name: Father, Son and Holy Spirit. Then instruct them in the practice of all I have commanded you.

As we go about life, doing what we do every day, and in the normal stuff we do, we are to make disciples. The call to share the Gospel of Jesus Christ with the world is to be part of the life we lead, part of what we do, not something we should to make plans to do. Evangelism is not what we plan to do for outsiders but what flows out of our lives. This is the reason I emphasize three missional rhythms of group life. Everything we do as a community has the potential to be missional.

• Missional Communion: When we learn to pray as a part of our life together and do it in a way that others can see, this is part of our witness. We don't pray so that people will see us, but we don't hide the way to connect to God from those outside the church. We let them see our relationship with God.

• Missional Relating: How we love one another is one of the most important witnessing tools we possess. To live in self-sacrificial way where we honor others more than ourselves will stand out in our culture.

• Missional Engagement: This last rhythm is about having conversations with people in our neighborhoods, listening to them to the point that they are heard and loved for who they are, not because they are a project to be won over.

The mission to share Jesus' Good News with the world is *not* simply something we do externally after we do our insider stuff. Our mission is to live the life of the Good News so that others can see.

prescribing missiorelate

Twelve years ago, I worked with Jim Egli to develop a holistic perspective of small groups called Upward, Inward, Outward, Forward (UIOF). We used this to differentiate our group training from groups that focus on just one or two of these things. The goal of this vision was to encourage groups that facilitate holistic organic life together and are not dependent upon more promotion tactics, curriculum, or a specific interest or task. It was our way of helping groups look outside of themselves and become missional.

Traditional small groups typically focus on one experience of the Christian life. Bible study groups meet to grow together in biblical knowledge. Discipleship groups meet to hold one another accountable and deepen their walk with Christ. Leadership groups meet around leadership issues. Service groups meet to do the specific task they've committed to accomplish. Evangelism groups meet to win the lost. Fellowship groups meet to develop and deepen friendship. Additional experiences are a hopeful by-product of the primary experience of the chosen focus of a group.

Holistic small groups aren't limited to one aspect of life in Christ. They're more than a group that meets to discuss the Bible. When Christ is in the midst of a group, the Bible will come to life. They're more than a discipleship group. When Christ is in the midst, discipleship will naturally occur. They're more than a group that does evangelism or works to accomplish a task. When a group focuses on Christ in the midst, the group will reach out to the lost and will work together in projects. The form a group takes is a by-product of the focus on Christ.

Christ manifests himself in groups through four experiences

The best way to define the experiences of a holistic group is found in the Great Commandment and the Great Commission. These two teachings of Jesus describe the essence of what small groups should experience, no matter what form they take.

First of all, holistic groups reach *Upward*: "Love the Lord your God with all of your heart, with all of your mind and with all of your strength."[2] These groups function powerfully because they focus on the living presence of God in the midst of the group. They're not 'fellowship' groups or Bible studies that meet for the sake of being together once per week. The members of these groups have a primary purpose: connecting to God.

Second, holistic groups reach *Inward*: "Love your neighbor as yourself."[3] Loving one another, encouraging one another, forgiving one another, showing hospitality to one another, and exhorting one another, are examples of New Testament commands for life in the church.

Small group members embrace these commands after they realize a group is far more than a weekly meeting. Some have even labeled holistic small groups as 'Sunday sermon groups' because many churches instruct groups to apply the Sunday sermon in their group meetings. But if a group is seen as only a meeting where a topic is discussed, then it will fail, regardless of what is discussed.

Third, holistic groups embrace the Great Commission by reaching *Outward*: "Go and preach the Gospel, baptizing them in the name of the Father, the Son and the Holy Spirit."[4] Healthy small groups demonstrate the gospel in such a way that the world can see Christ in them. They graciously invite people a relational place where they can find Christ and the love in the midst of community.

Finally, holistic groups move *Forward*: "teaching them to observe everything I have commanded you."[5] It's not enough for group members to attend a meeting every week. The ultimate goal is for them to advance in their relationship with the Lord, becoming more like him. We move Forward as we are discipled in the ways of Upward, Inward and Outward. This will result in developing new group leaders who lead new small groups.

The diagram on the following page illustrates how the four values of Upward, Inward, Outward, and Forward work together in the development of healthy and holistic small groups:

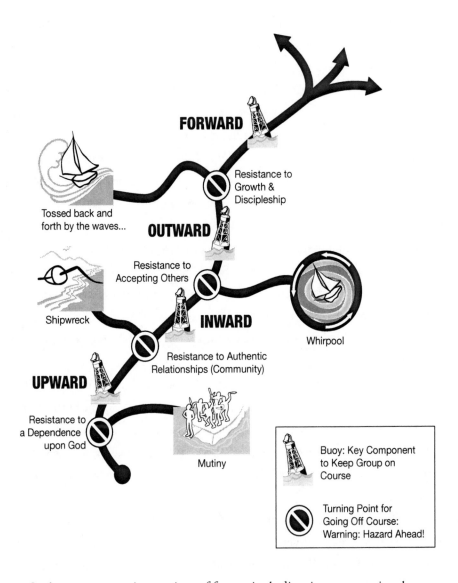

FORWARD

Resistance to Growth & Discipleship

Tossed back and forth by the waves...

OUTWARD

Resistance to Accepting Others

Shipwreck

INWARD

Whirpool

Resistance to Authentic Relationships (Community)

UPWARD

Resistance to a Dependence upon God

Mutiny

Buoy: Key Component to Keep Group on Course

Turning Point for Going Off Course: Warning: Hazard Ahead!

Such groups come in a variety of forms, including intergenerational groups that meet in homes. They also include men's groups, women's groups, and youth groups. They include groups that meet during lunch breaks in office buildings or parks, groups where workers meet at midnight after their shift ends, young mothers' groups that meet on Tuesday mornings, collegiate groups that meet in dorm rooms, and newly married couples' groups that meet on Saturday nights. The form UIOF holistic small groups can take is unlimited.

I remain convinced that UIOF groups provide the best MissioRelate experience for people. When I have participated or led groups like these, they have resulted in far more life transformation and impact outside the group than any other small group from my past. However, I've learned to talk about UIOF groups a little differently than I did when I was working full-time as a consultant. With more pastoral experience under my belt today, I have observed a consistent response to UIOF—no one disagrees with it in principle. How could they? It's so biblical. In fact, leaders and groups will affirm it with all of their being, but then they struggle or fail when they attempt to do it.

The UIOF definitions seek to bring clarity to what we are aiming to produce in the life of our groups: The Great Commandment and The Great Commission. The problem isn't the content. It's the delivery. Church leaders have a bad habit of telling people what they should do in their groups by prescribing external goals, expecting them to live up to those goals. As a result, we encourage groups to participate in life together outside the group meetings but they end up being "meeting groups." We tell groups to serve their communities and evangelize the lost, but they don't adopt it as a way of life. We urge groups to multiply when they grow numerically, but they end of staying together for years. It's frustrating for everyone, from the pastor to the group leader and even those group members who understand the need for all four directional values of missional group life.

What can we do to change this pattern?

We could meet with leaders and challenge them to live up to the vision of UIOF. Or, we could entice them to do UIOF with rewards or recognition. Then we could shut down any group that does not actually do UIOF and multiply at a certain rate. These are only external motivators. We must embrace a way to encourage groups into UIOF with internal motivation. If we can facilitate the life of the Spirit of God within groups to stir people to live UIOF on their own, we won't feel the urge to force MissioRelate (which can't be forced upon a group anyway). By internal encouragement, we become facilitators of MissioRelate so it can develop in many organic and creative forms.

a shift in language = a shift in imagination

In some ways, UIOF correlates with the pattern of Missional Communion, Missional Relating and Missional Engagement. In other ways, I am promoting something distinctive. I have shifted away from a prescriptive imagination to what I call "an imagination of discovery." Instead of telling groups what they should be doing—implying that if they don't they're not welcome—I seek to help people discover a path toward missional life by answering questions that are central to how we do life.

The power behind self-discovery is that it frees us to create environments based on powerful questions instead of prescribed, top-down patterns developed by leadership. If we work within the big questions about life and personal significance people are already asking, we will encounter less resistance. Groups within all four stories become places where we talk about big life questions:

- Who am I?
- Where do I belong?
- What can I contribute? (How can I impact this world?)
- What's the next step on my journey with God?

By inviting people in our groups to answer these four questions, their answers will shape the forms of life together that will move them from normal into a MissoRelate group. Instead of stating that group membership will look a certain way, we can teach people these questions and walk with them as they ask and answer these questions for themselves, one another, and God. As we do this, our groups will have an opportunity to think holistically about the ways they connect. There's also a bonus: members take ownership in the life of the group more quickly because they are being challenged to answer their own questions rather than questions given to them by the leadership of the church.

Of course, groups that are living out a Personal Improvement or Lifestyle Adjustment story will answer these questions in a very self-focused or individualistic way. However, as they engage in Spirit-directed dialogue, they will discover other possibilities. The key is to continue asking these questions in creative ways.

As we help groups work through these questions and discover what it takes to move from the normal group stories to missional stories, we will see how the questions can be modified or rephrased. Then, as the group enters into life with one another on deeper levels, we will discover and embrace the differences in people around them. This becomes even more apparent as we enter into conversations with people in our neighborhoods. Just don't anticipate how or when a group will manifest MissioRelate stories. Here's a surprising personal story about this very issue.

Immersed in life questions

My wife and I were part of a group that met for ten weeks around the issue of serving "the poor." This was an experimental group that included people from different socioeconomic experiences. Some were from a middle class background; some were raised in generational poverty; one person spent a significant time in jail; and another was a successful businessman who had lost everything in the recession.

As we moved through the material, the conversations were transforming. Our new found friends—whom the curriculum labeled as "the poor"—revealed my misconceptions about this group. They would say things such as, "This book calls people 'the poor', but I don't see myself as part of 'the poor.' We don't sit on our porches in the inner city talking about how poor we are." In other words, that label was categorically unfair. They did not want us socially well-to-do Christians labeling them and telling them how they should live. I will never forget when one person said, "We don't want your money. If all you want to do is give us money, keep it. If you are interested in interacting with us by learning and talking, then you will find no resistance to that." In a similar vein another person stated, "I have no desire to own a home or become middle-class." He didn't want the "good" life, which he viewed as a rat-race filled with stress and unnecessary pressure.

In response to the book's instructions to middle class people driving to a "poor" neighborhood and walking around to observe what was going on, one person said, "Do you want to get hurt? That's just stupid." As we unpacked the comment, it became obvious that Christ is not well represented when middle-class suburbanites walk around an economically under-resourced neighborhood so that they can "minister to it."

Through these conversations, I realized that if we are going to effectively minister to the "poor" we needed a new imagination, one that shifted us away from thinking that we had something to give to those who are under-resourced. Instead of setting the table and inviting them to eat with us, we needed to learn to set the table together and share what each of us brings to that table. The same is true of all kinds of people who are not a part of our churches or small groups. We have plenty of programs for ministering to outsiders. We have more than enough evangelism strategies for explaining the plan of salvation. What we need more is conversational patterns where we learn to ask MissioRelate questions:

- Who am I? Who are we? Who is God and what does that have to do with me and our life as a group? (revealing Missional Communion)

- Where do I belong? Who is my spiritual family? What does this family look like under God's direction? (revealing Missional Relating)

- What can I offer this world? What can we do today to bring beauty into ugliness in this world? What is God asking me and us to do right now? (revealing Missional Engagement)

- What is our next step on the journey? What is God calling this group to do differently? How can we be prepared for that next leg? (revealing Missional Formation)

As a pastor, part of my job is to facilitate environments where we can explore these questions together. I don't have to determine all of the structures, curriculum, and strategies to make groups work. If I can get people asking the questions above in their groups, they will come up with transformational answers. This is crucial to the meaning of being on mission in North America: experimenting and developing new patterns of missional living. This is the point of the next chapter. The point I want to leave you with here is that we cannot prescribe how the experience of missional community will unfold. Dynamic organic life of this kind is alive and must be discovered.

On the reflection pages that follow, write down your thoughts about these questions: As you read this chapter, what was your immediate reaction? Have you been leading from a prescriptive way? How have you been taught that good leadership is prescriptive? How does the skill of asking good questions change the way you must lead in the future? Listen to your heart. What is going on as you reflect on this?

missiorelate

*An experience with others and God
that makes a difference in the world*

encourage
experiments

I n the summer of 2005, my wife and I
packed a large yellow truck, loaded up
our two boys (both under three years old
at the time) and left the security of home,
family, friends, and a church that loved us
. . . and the great state of Texas. I accepted
an invitation to serve as one of the pastors
at Woodland Hills Church, entering a time
of radical unpredictability and transition as
we abandoned all-things-familiar for our
new home in Saint Paul, Minnesota. This
Texas-born family was moving to the land
of six-month winters and unusual accents,
even though they think Texans talk funny.
Our learning curve about life and ministry in
America had just taken a sharp incline.

My relationship with Woodland Hills developed over the previous three
years. The leaders read my books on small groups and brought me in a couple
of times for training events. This led them to hire me to lead them into what
they found in my books.

Although I was hired to lead the vision in the area of my expertise, I began
my new job by seeking what God was already doing through his people at
Woodland Hills. In many ways, I assumed that what I would find would be a
natural next step of what I had already been doing. In some ways it was, but
in other ways, it was a radical departure adding to my experience of unpredictability and transition. What I saw God doing through the people did not fit

well with the model of small group life and structures that were currently in place at Woodland Hills. This disconnect brought about a new discovery surrounding the power and unpredictability of experiments.

The tendency of both consultants and decisive leaders is to develop a structure for achieving a vision and then ask people to get involved in that structure. People want answers, but I felt led to ask questions anyway. And this led to the different perspective of helping people answer their questions that I introduced in the previous chapter.

I knew that I was taking a risk. Some would surely see me as indecisive or not having clear answers. But the only thing I knew I could decisively do at that point was to *listen*. I knew that I was not to judge what I thought would not fit and require people to line up with the small group structure in place. If it concerned any other issue, I had to just trust God. So I listened. Here's what I heard:

I *like our groups!*

There were a lot of people who liked doing small groups according to the plan. They wanted to lead groups by the book and follow the direction of the leadership. I discovered that the structure of Woodland Hills, shaped by what I wrote in my books, fit these people quite well. These people were at the center of the structure, but I realized that they were only living the story of Lifestyle Adjustment.

I *like groups, but not the official church groups.*

There was another segment of people who participated in small groups but were not part of the system. They believed in the crucial role of small group life, but they did not feel the need to get involved with the direction of the church's official small group vision. Some of these people did not see a benefit of participating in the structure, so they operated outside it to do their own thing. Others just felt led to do group life differently and it didn't fit within the constraints of our system. Because these groups did not fit, these groups were viewed as "vapor" groups. The leadership of the sanctioned small group system judged them for being independent. But I saw God at work through these groups. Most were doing Lifestyle Adjustment just like the groups that lined up, but we had no relationship with them and we could not help them go further.

I'm not yet ready for group life.

Then I discovered a large segment of our church comprised of those who wanted to participate in group life but were not ready to do so. Their reasons varied, but a few of the patterns became obvious. The relational leap from the Sunday worship to the small group was just too big for some. It was unnatural to jump from the formal public gathering to the personal space of someone's home. Others were in a life-stage that made the existing groups an unnatural fit. A third group revealed that, due to past relationship experiences, they were not in a place where they could enter into the relational connections found in group life in a healthy way.

Sunday is all the church I need, thank you very much.

Finally, there was a large group of attendees to a weekend service who had no desire to participate in community. To these individuals, a Sunday service in the building was church, no matter what we said. And what we delivered to these people was a satisfactory Sunday church experience. From their perspective, they did not need or want any more church in a more intimate setting.

on the edge

There was one other significant group of people that did not fit. The only way to explain this is to tell four stories of missional people at Woodland Hills that were not a part of our small group system or mentioned above.

Kent and I met for lunch. He served as a group leader in the past at our church but was not currently in leadership. Before participating in our church, he was the volunteer small group point person at another church. He was well-versed in small groups from extensive reading and even traveled oversees to observe what some of the most creative churches were doing with groups. As I listened to his story, I wondered why he was not being utilized in our groups system. Then he shared what he was presently doing. He was leading a team who facilitated the Alpha course every Wednesday night at the Salvation Army in Minneapolis. Most of the men at the "Sali" (his abbreviated term) were in a transitional situation as they had recently been released from the county jail. Some of the men that "graduated" from the Sali would participate in a house owned by an non-profit ministry where Kent led a weekly house church meeting. My immediate thought was, "This does not fit our group structure, but shouldn't it? Why is it the case when someone really hears God that they have to go and start a new organization to do it?"

Sandra launched the small groups ministry at Woodland over a decade before my arrival. She had subsequently been on the staff of two of the largest churches in North America and then returned to the Twin Cities to work in the inner city in an economically under-resourced neighborhood. As a part of her ministry, she began a small group with women from her neighborhood, individuals who would most likely never attend our weekend services. Again, I asked, "Why is it that someone who belongs to our church has to operate outside the church system to accomplish the kingdom vision?"

Tim was leader in the church who had a passion for the geographic area where he lived. After moving into his home, he adopted his street and lived life with the people who lived nearby. At the time we first met and spoke about his relational connection to his neighbors, he was not participating in one of our small groups, which I naturally questioned. But when I listened, I found that I needed to wait and see what God would do on Tim's street. After many long conversations with Tim, a retired couple caught a vision to live more simply. So they sold their home and moved two houses away from Tim and his wife. The four of them have established a ministry core to those who live on their block. The members of his small group live within walking distance, even though none of them attend our church or any other church for that matter. I wondered. "How is God working through this unique situation and how can we learn from this so that our groups can capture this 'out-of-the-box' imagination?"

The last story is about a guy named Ken. He would often talk about his house church that met every Saturday night, often going into the wee hours of the morning. This group has been living in community, praying for each other, and his house church members were connected to ministries in Haiti. When asked why he or another one of the group's leaders were not coming to the various support meetings that we were providing, his response was "How would that help us do what God is calling us to do?" At first, I judged what seemed like arrogance, but as I listened more to what they were doing, I realized that his honest response was dead on. But again, it made me think about why we had no room in our small group imagination for one of our best and most creative leaders.

These are four stories of small groups led by people who belonged to our church, but did not fit into our structure. After the interviews with these people (where I just listened) I realized I had three responsive choices:

- Choose a high control system and mandate how groups would be done.
- Choose a low control system and accept everything we saw going on small group-wise.
- Continue to listen to what God was doing and then develop a system to provide the appropriate direction and support for the appropriate people.

Of course, the last option became the only real option, even though it was the most difficult one to embrace. Choosing this option has led to many difficult conversations among the leadership of the church. It has forced us to wrestle with the creative and out-of-control ways that the Spirit of God leads people into MissioRelate and respond accordingly. At the same time, we have carefully examined the more typical small groups, those considered to be the center of our system, asking God how he is moving.

It has become clear to me that God is moving through small groups that fit into almost any church small group system if the leaders in that system don't force the groups to look, act, and feel like all the other groups in their system. As a result, instead of arguing for the old system of control versus the organic, anything-goes system, we are seeking to listen to the Spirit to develop a system that works with what God is already doing.

participating in the Spirit who dwells in our midst

To actually embrace the third option has required that we truly lead according the fact that the Spirit resides in and amongst us in our groups, even when we don't fully see or understand what the Spirit is doing. When we accept this truth about the Spirit, group life then moves far beyond meetings, studying curriculum, or fulfilling the expectations established by church leaders. The Spirit fills the group with life. Peter tells us that we are "participants in the divine nature" (2 Peter 1:4). God's nature is love. And as the Spirit comes to live in a group that is moving from normal into MissioRelate, the life and love of a group will move it to the fringes. The group will take on new ways of existing and operating.

As we participate in the Holy Spirit with others, we are participants in his love. Love is not something that can be prescribed in a book or through a teaching session. Love is creative in nature. Each situation where love comes to life will be unique, just as every story about a group that moves into some kind of MissioRelate experience is unique. The Spirit carries the love of God out beyond the bounds of what we expect, into our neighborhoods, inside our families, at the workplace, and among friends.

This is why I don't prescribe a form for a missional small group. Practices should be introduced that a normal group can adopt together as they embrace the story of Relational Revision. These practices teach them the ways of the Spirit that moves in the life of the community. Then, as these practices become regular group patterns, the Spirit leads them to the creative fringes, to the unexpected, to experiment.

learning from experiments on the fringe

Most churches choose what they will endorse. The creative ones—often called emergent or organic—embrace what is happening at the edges or fringes of the Christian Church. They meet in creative ways and in creative places like those listed above, meeting in pubs or coffee houses with unique interactive Bible discussion that does not fit with traditional forms of sermons or Bible studies.

Established churches usually focus on the center of the Christian church, seeking to connect those who attend their traditional church services. But do we need to choose between the two? By choosing to focus only on the center, we miss the results of experiments that could lead to engagement with the neighborhood.

On the fringes of the church, you'll find the innovators and entrepreneurs or those who enjoy experimentation. The problem is that they are usually disconnected from those at the center: people who are more stable and actually have the ability to complete the journey and carry out successful experiments to completion. So instead of conversations across the boundaries, like persons relate to like persons and the division grows.

Those at the center need those on the fringes to open up new paths and test new perspectives. Those on the fringes need those at the center to keep them grounded and accountable so that we are no longer just creating new ideas for the sake of new ideas.

No church can embrace a single way to successfully promote missional community. Our context is always changing and new experiments are always needed. And we need those who are more stable to carry out the experiments to fruitful life.

effectively exposing people to missiorelate

God sends his church on mission in this world to incarnate the life of Christ as God's people. Every church has a center and a fringe. MissioRelate requires an imagination that empowers all kinds of people to embark on this mission. It would be much easier to say that the innovators on the fringe should simply start new churches and that those at the center of church life should just remain in the established structures of the church. But I believe that both are necessary in every congregation, no matter the size. Let's look at why this is the case by thinking about how people process new ideas.

Different people will process the new idea of MissioRelate in different ways. Some respond well to new ideas and change, while others need more time and information before they embrace it. There are five basic responses to change.[1] The diagram below shows the size of each group, followed by a detailed explanation:[2]

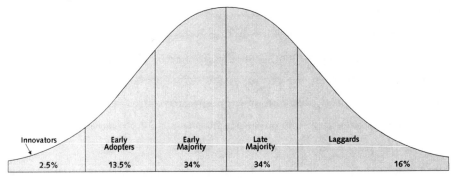

Innovators	Early Adopters	Early Majority	Late Majority	Laggards
2.5%	13.5%	34%	34%	16%

Innovators

These people are obsessed with being venturesome. They challenge the status quo and expand the current boundaries by introducing new ideas. While not all of their ideas are practical or workable, their concern is to explore new territory. Innovators make many mistakes because they will adopt new ideas simply because they are new.

Innovators are able to visualize a new idea without ever seeing it. They do not need to increase their dissatisfaction with current reality, because they are always dissatisfied with the old. They continually feel a sense of urgency and embrace change just because it is change. To introduce a new idea to an innovator, a simple meeting is often sufficient, followed up with some reading material.

Early Adopters

These people are characterized by respectability. They are ahead of the pack, but not too far ahead. Therefore, they have the greatest degree of influence upon others in the church.

The vision cannot survive without the Early Adopters. These are the people who can understand what the Innovators are doing and then turn the new idea into action. Many times, it is best for Early Adopters to see the vision in another church, either through a conference or through a case study book. Honest discussion about current reality, with the help of assessment tools, will often develop a sense of urgency in an early adopter. They will need time, but it will pay off in the long run.

Early Majority

These people are deliberate individuals who make up one third of the population. They adhere to the motto, "Be not the first by which the new is tried, nor the last to lay the old aside." They will follow with deliberate willingness, but they will seldom lead.

It takes longer for members of the Early Majority to develop urgency. They need time to process current reality and a leader who will make them feel safe in this process. They have a limited ability to understand a new vision by reading about it or seeing it at another church. Primarily they need to experience it in order to adopt it. They will follow people they trust into a new vision and then they will take it on as their own.

Late Majority

Making up another third of the population, these people view new ideas with skepticism and caution. The pressure of peers and obvious circumstantial pointers must lead them to see the necessity of change before they will change.

Because those in the Late Majority category only adopt a new idea after other people are doing it and thereby proving it successful, pastors cannot expect this group to feel much urgency until they see it working in their church. To see small groups working in another church is not enough.

Laggards

These are the last to adopt new ideas, as they are traditional and their reference point is in the past. They tend to be suspicious of the new and those who promote new ideas. This group rarely feels an urgency to change until they see that the small group train has left the station and they realize that they are being left behind. They will change only because everyone else has changed.

In most cases it is not hard to identify those who fall into the Innovator or Early Adopter categories. They are often those who are never satisfied even when things are going well. They are reading books that talk about things differently and seeking new ways to do things. These are the people who need to lead the charge with experimenting.

These people are usually not the stakeholders who sit in positions of power in a church. The stakeholders are typically stable, centered people who usually fall into the middle adopter categories. If that is the case, those people don't particularly like experimenting with new ideas.[3] It is crucial to establish clear communication and a working relationship between those doing the experimentation and the stakeholders on the church board, but to force the board to commit to figuring out new ideas is counterproductive. And to change the board so that experimenters can have the power is equally frustrating. No innovative company puts those good at research and development in charge of the daily decisions. But if the research is going to be productive, the two groups must learn how to communicate with one another.

examples of missiorelate experiments

Alan Roxburgh is a collaborative colleague and he's given a great deal of thought when thinking about structures that are engaging their neighborhoods. He offers these six options that can help church leaders when working with innovative leaders:[4]

1. Initiation structures

This structure is designed for the seeker or immature believer. For a period of up to a year, three to five initiates would meet with a mentor who would lead them through a series of teaching about the life and work of Jesus. Through a dialogue around Jesus, the initiates would discover implications shared by Jesus on how they live their lives. This process is not shaped by a specific curriculum or teaching content. It is dependant upon a face-to-face relationship with a wise, discerning mentor, focused on listening and offering guidance for his/her formation in Christian life.

2. Table gatherings

The basic pattern is a regular (weekly or biweekly) gathering around the meal of a group of Christians living in proximity to one another. Over meals they can share their lives, pray for one another and their neighborhood. Also, this is the place where people talk about ways God is leading them to practice hospitality in the neighborhood.

3. Training modules

At times the leadership of the church might find the need to gather the community together for brief periods of training and teaching (several weeks in duration). There are some things that can be discussed and learned in the regular rhythms of small group life, but at times it is very effective to break the pattern and invite groups to gather so that they can think "outside the box." These trainings should be identified out of the interaction and life in the neighborhoods. For instance, gathering people to practice table gatherings can be an effective way to launch such group experiences.

4. 'Coffee table' gatherings

The metaphor of the coffee table suggests a safe, welcoming space where friends meet to listen and talk together. Here is how it works: Two or three times a year, the community comes together as a whole to listen and talk with one another around two questions:

- What is God up to in the neighborhoods and communities where our church members live?
- What might be the ways God is calling us as a whole church to shape ourselves in order to join with God?

These gatherings are not times when leadership shares a plan or strategy. They are times when the local church practices discernment as a community, seeking to discover what the Spirit is saying to them at that moment in time. The role of leadership is to create a safe space for such dialogue.

5. 'Parish' structures

This might seem like an outdated concept rooted in European church life. This might feel even more foreign when you consider that people don't think about church in terms of location and place, but instead travel quite a distance to attend their church of preference. But being missional is about being local, recognizing what God is doing in a specific neighborhood.

The most mission-shaped, counter-cultural move a local church can make is to structure its life around a move of its members back into specific neighborhoods. The church moves from being a building where people gather to a center where people are empowered to see their neighborhood as their parish—the place where they belong, connect, live, eat, love, and welcome the stranger for the sake of the kingdom.

Such local churches see the neighborhoods where its people live as the centers of mission and life. What a local church would do, therefore, is re-introduce the idea of the parish for a neighborhood, four or five streets in urban areas, or an actual suburb in suburbia. These people would meet in table or mission groups in the name and for the sake of being God's people in that area. The local church, with its staff and building, would become a training, resourcing, and equipping center for its parishes and their ministries.

6. *Target-focused groups*

This kind of group is comprised of people who have come together around a specific need in their neighborhood. Examples might include: caring for latch-key kids; running a drop in-center or after-school education program; developing a child/parent program; working with unemployed youth in the area; launching programs and resources for the homeless and poor in the area; or embracing a specific ethnic group in an area. Such groups are supported by a covenant that spells out what it means to belong and participate. It will shape itself around a basic rule of life and a set of practices, while always keeping focused on its mission covenant. As I stated earlier, groups may find that they need to combine forces with a few other groups in a local neighborhood in order to effectively fulfill this mission. Another approach might be to rethink the size of the group. In a specific context, it might be more effective for the group to gather as 20-50 people and then have subgroups within that larger group in order to facilitate more personal sharing.

The focus of these experiments is two-fold. First, the experimenters must consider their context, or to put it another way, they must seek to understand the people "in the neighborhood." This is far beyond the idea of trying to find a way of doing church for church people. One very large church in Ohio began down this path by leaving all of their current small groups in place, but identified key leaders who were willing to try something new. They equipped and supported them, but they did not give them people from the church. They were given the challenge to start home groups with people who would not come to church through the front door. Each week, these home group leaders are given a DVD of the pastor's sermon, which they watch in their homes and discuss in groups. These leaders were challenged to think about their neighbors, unchurched friends, family members, and coworkers to create the kind of group that would meet their needs and desires.

The second focus is on listening to the Spirit. The Spirit of God moves out ahead of us. If we listen and ask for the ability to discern what is going on, leaders will come up with creative ways to engage their neighborhoods. Get ready, you might not be comfortable with all of these experiments. Some will invariably fail. But this is the only way you will learn. There is no "MissioRelate in a box" that works in every context. We must depend upon the Spirit.

On the following pages reflect on your thoughts that arose as you read this chapter. What was your first reaction to the need to let go of control? How have you responded to out-of the-box thinking in the past? How do you respond to people who don't follow the rules all the time? How could you work with such people differently?

missiorelate
*An experience with others and God
that makes a difference in the world*

equip people in relational intelligence

A few years ago I was a part of a gathering with small group pastors from some of the largest churches in North America. It was an impressive array of what I call "smallgroupologists." In one activity, we were divided up into groups of four to brainstorm projects that we thought were important for small group life in America. We wrote down each project on a large piece of paper and then hung it on a wall for everyone to see.

At my table, we went around the circle and contributed our ideas, but I withheld the one I thought to be the most important. I assumed that no one there would need such a resource. Their group systems were successful and they wouldn't need this resource. Eventually I could not contain myself and asked, "What about a resource or curriculum that equipped the average American in basic relational skills?" The person recording the ideas on paper was a former counselor and his eyes grew wide with interest. He wrote on the top of the page "Relational Intelligence Curriculum."

After each subgroup posted our giant Post-it® notes on the wall, we were each given five dots to stick on the ideas that we felt were most important. To my surprise, the relational intelligence idea got the most dots. Evidently I was not alone.

Over the last few years, I have led hundreds of people through a process of seeing how they do life and relationships. Rather than telling them that the typical American is relatively unskilled at relating to others (which is a rather nice way to state it), I've found it more effective to invite them into a self-discovery process.

Here's how it works. I invite them to imagine that they are in a conversation with a historian 200 years from now. She is writing a book on America in the early years of the twenty-first century. Her research is not delving into the history of war or politics, which is the normal stuff for history classes. She is focusing on everyday life to determine how people lived.

When I ask the group, "What words might she use to describe how we live today?" the participants shout out statements such as:

- Fast-paced, frenzied, time-crunched
- Lonely, isolated,
- Productive
- Unsettled, transient
- Television
- Extended family scattered

- Controlled by fear
- Fast-food
- Exciting, exhilarating
- Technology-driven
- Rootless

Then I ask the group to write words that this historian might use to describe how people "do relationships" today. The list always includes statements or terms such as:

- Avoidance of Conflict
- We have too many
- Overwhelming
- Social media-driven (Facebook and Twitter)

- Paper-thin
- Surface
- Short-term
- Nice

One person responded after offering her perspective, "Are there any *positive* aspects to the way we live today?" This led us to a conversation around central heat (I live in Minnesota after all), SUVs, email, education, medical advancements, freedom from tyranny (in some places), and for some, the option to choose one's profession. We were hard pressed to find positive aspects of modern life that have made our relationships better.

It's obvious to most everyone that we need help relating to one another. It's not enough to teach people the importance of obeying the "one anothers" (love one another, encourage one another, bless one another, serve one another, and so forth). Telling them what they should be doing without equipping them for the task is like sending a student home with homework without teaching them how to complete it. As I write this, I reflect on so many small group experiences where there were great hopes and dreams of how the community could be empowered to impact others. These groups fell short because they did not know how to do some of the basic things to make their own relationships work well.

What we can learn from those outside the small group world

My colleague Kevin Calligan is a licensed Christian counselor. Through the years, he has worked with people ranging from the chronically ill to those who just need an emotional tune-up. And of course, there have been numerous couples who have come to him for counseling. In his work with couples, he realized that the skills they did not possess were the same basic skills needed to make any relationship healthy. Gary Smalley came to the same conclusion in his book, *The DNA of Relationships*. He writes, "The exciting concepts and methods hammered out in our marriage intensives apply to all relationships, not merely to marriage. I made this discovery for myself as I saw major improvements taking place in my home and with friends."[1] The difference is that it's socially acceptable to seek out and receive relational training for the sake of our marriages. We just don't think about a need to be trained to relate to one another in our friendships.

The work of sociologists Will Miller and Glen Sparks has focused on cultural patterns that undermine social connectivity in American life. They have identified mundane cultural patterns that are shaping how we live and are much more basic than the broad category of individualism. In their work, they pinpoint things like: the average American watches 28-34 hours of television per week; the alarming rate of relocation of the American family; and the extended length of the average workweek. Such patterns shape the lives of the average American church attendee more than the story of the Bible, the way of the cross, or the practice of silence and solitude. Miller and Sparks are speaking about the basic disciplines of the American life. For the church in North America to successfully develop a people that live out the kingdom of God, then we must call out these American disciplines for what they are. Our current struggle with small group ministry has clearly shown we cannot superimpose practices of the kingdom over the practices of the American way.[2]

In Romans 12:1-2, Paul wrote, "Therefore, I urge you, brothers and sisters, in view of God's mercy, to offer your bodies as a living sacrifice, holy and pleasing to God—this is your true and proper worship. Do not conform to the pattern of this world, but be transformed by the renewing of your mind. Then you will be able to test and approve what God's will is—his good, pleasing and perfect will." This passage is often applied to moral issues like promiscuity or drug usage. The prevailing argument is that the rhythms of this world are immoral and those of God are moral. While I recognize that morality is certainly part of the rhythmic differences, we can't stop there or we miss the point of love. Without the love of God, we will make following Jesus into a lifestyle of avoidance and fail to see what the dance is really about.

There are many cultural patterns of life that are so common today that they simply go unquestioned by the church. These include but are not limited to consumerism, individualism, and isolationism. Just these three have created a cultural pattern that has progressively advanced since the 1950s. This gradual focus on the advancement of the individual, coupled with the need to be perceived as being successful (which usually means buying lots of stuff) has eroded the value of relationships with friends and family.

This is easy enough to agree with until we talk about it in practical terms that confront the idolization of a consumer-driven Christmas. Then it gets personal! And what about how we assume that job advancement, more money, and a bigger home are more important than any dream God has for us? And finally, what we call a good work ethic is simply an excuse to hide behind our work so we don't have to do relationships. Workaholism is a cake walk compared to relating to others deeply.

These examples are simply patterns of life that our culture elevates as important. To challenge them raises questions such as, "What else would we do for Christmas if we didn't buy gifts for the kids? They'd feel so left out." Or, "Why wouldn't I go for the better paying job? I'm worth it and we need the money." Or, "If I don't put in 65 hours a week then someone else will. Haven't you heard about the layoffs?"

Challenging the norms of a culture is a formidable endeavor. The questions are hard to raise and the answers are even more difficult to find. There are some that think it is easy, but when we look at life plainly and honestly most of the issues are difficult to address. Even if we look at something like consumerism and we recognize the hold it has one our lives and we make a plan to change things, the fact remains that we live in a consumerist society. Unless the plan includes becoming a hermit, it will prove impossible to avoid being influenced by this cultural pattern.

I just saw a new book by a Christian leader[3] which challenges people to put down roots in a community and stay put for the long haul. We live in a transient society where the average person moves once every four years, which is not long enough to establish a presence in a community and invest in the lives of people. But even when we make commitments to put down roots, it remains difficult because most people that live near you will be moving sooner than later.

If we don't enter a different dance, we will be conformed to the patterns of this world. This word "conformed" is one that refers to being shaped from the outside in. We are conformed to a mold that is set from the outside and that mold makes us. And if we don't choose otherwise, this mold will shape us even when we don't realize it. Even Christians fall prey to being conformed to the mold of the world. After all, Paul's letter to the Romans was written to Christians. One of the biggest traps that Satan sets is based on the thought that we need not be concerned with being like the world. Satan actually tells us that all we need to do is relax and let transformation take its natural course. The truth is that transformation does not work that way. The dance of love will always be a "swimming upstream" experience in this world. It will be one characterized by resisting the status quo and won't be something that lots of people will chose to embrace because of the sustained difficulty it guarantees.

four levels of training in relational intelligence

In chapter 9, I introduced basic questions that we must help people answer, one of which is, "Where do I belong?" Training people in Relational Intelligence is all about creating new ways for people to discover answers to this basic question. I believe that the realities that we face today in our context require all that we do to have a relational application. Sermons, worship, youth activities, and men's and women's events must be viewed through the lens of equipping people for relationships. We must never assume we can put people through a course and expect them to know how to relate. Our context begs us to address the need for healthy relating as a reoccurring theme.

There are specific ways we can focus on Relational Intelligence. I see four levels of training or ways that we can equip people to grow in their patterns of relating. In some ways, they are correlated to the four stories. The current stories lived out in your church or groups will impact which kinds of training you might incorporate.

Level 1: Making room training

I use this name because of the influence of Randy Frazee and his book *Making Room for Life*. In it he challenges specific patterns of American suburban living and provides alternatives that are practical and concrete. The point of it is to re-frame how we spend time and make room for relationships. It really does not matter if we have great relationship skills and have an overwhelming desire to connect with others if we don't have the time or space in our lives for people. A few years ago I wrote a six-week series entitled *The Beautiful Life*. It is a church-wide initiative to help people see the problem and begin to embrace a simpler life. We repeated this theme with another church-wide initiative about three years later entitled *Undivided*. Recently, Max Lucado and Randy Frazee have produced a small group curriculum piece called *Making Room for Neighbors*. Tools like this are really helpful to wake our people up to the fact that relationships won't just happen if we don't make room for them.

God is calling the church to a simple life that has room for love, not improved or even missional small groups. The complexity and chaos that rules life today is subtly eroding love. We were made for more than work, stress, and church activities. God did not design us to find life through small group meetings alone, as helpful as those might be. So much of what has been touted as "missional" fails to recognize this. How can we be on mission in this world when the way we do life really does not look that much different than the average moral American citizen? We might have a different message, but if that message has no tangible, practical impact on the now of our lives, we should not be surprised when our groups fail to make a difference. When we make room for relationships, we realize that we are actually starting to live the way we were designed to live.

Level 2: Basic skills training

When I was a teenager, I participated in 4-H and FFA. While much of what we did was centered around our agriculture projects, there was another side to these organizations that city dwellers don't see. These organizations emphasize the importance of learning good social skills. I don't remember going to any kind of formal training, but I do recall how I learned the basics like how to introduce myself to others, how to show interest in people and get to know them, and how to work as a team to make decisions together. At one retreat, we learned the finer details of table manners and tips for remembering people's names (although I still struggle with that one).

These things might not sound very important compared to what is typically considered as spiritual. You'll change your mind when you stop and realize how many people don't possess these basic social skills today. While what I learned in 4-H and FFA is usually used by people to get ahead in this world, the skills are just as important when you are trying to serve others sacrificially. The basic relational skills taught by Dale Carnegie over 70 years ago in his book, *How To Win Friends and Influence People,* hold true if you are trying to sell cars or enter into community. After all, Paul instructed the churches at Rome and Corinth to greet one another with a holy kiss! How we interact socially has ramifications upon how we love one another as a community. If we greet well, the doors will open to deeper connections.

If you stop to ponder it, many of the one another passages are reminders about how we should treat each other socially. As I stated above, we just need the skill training to do this well. Specifically, people in our churches and groups need to process:

- How to greet another person when they come into a room.
- How to ask questions of a person to get to know them.
- How to listen to another person.
- How to invite a few people to your home for a meal and make them feel welcome.
- How to share life with people who are significantly different in personality and interest.
- How to relate to people from different ethnic backgrounds.

Relational conflict cannot be avoided in group life. Every valuable group leader training book I've reviewed addresses this topic. Additionally, almost every book I've written has stated something about group conflict. Conflict is the great mountain range that keeps people from the Promised Land. If groups are not prepared for it, they cannot endure the rough terrain. The fact is that we don't need to train our leaders more in how to navigate conflict, or "manage" it—a concept beyond me. As I stated earlier, by the time a group enters into conflict, it's too late to equip them to effectively deal with it. When someone is frustrated or even angry at another group member, they don't want to hear something like, "You know what you are experiencing is normal. This is called the "conflict stage' of group life."

A few years ago, I wrote a six-week, church-wide initiative called *The Beautiful Mess*. Through this, we realized the importance of preparing people about conflict long before they actually face the emotions of it. We found that much of the conflict was already there, laying dormant under the surface of relationships. People need to know what it is, where it comes from, how to respond to it, and make a commitment to work through it. Without such a game-plan, conflict kills far too many groups.

Level 3: Growing in love

For some reason, church for me has never been something that I have attempted to pile on top of or add to my normal life. Early on as a kid, I realized that if I was going to take Jesus seriously, it created ramifications in every area of my life. It was not enough to get saved so I could be prepared to go to Heaven. For some reason, I knew that discipleship for living today was important.

In some ways this makes total sense because I am an "all-or-nothing" type of person who is a bit intense and sometimes overly serious. In addition, I love to learn. So disciplines like Bible study, reading books, memorizing scriptures, and the development of leadership skills just fits my personality. The problem was that for much of my early life, discipleship for the sake of discipleship was the goal. I was laboring to grow in all aspects of discipleship for the sake of being a better disciple.

Recently I realized that this focus on discipleship for the sake of discipleship is akin to running in circles. Discipleship must be for the sake of something else, not an end in itself. I have repeatedly referenced the importance of discipleship or formation in previous chapters, and I will return to a different aspect of it in chapter 13. Here I want to identify the goal of discipleship: growth in love.

> I pray that out of his glorious riches he may strengthen you with power through his Spirit in your inner being, so that Christ may dwell in your hearts through faith. And I pray that you, being rooted and established in love, may have power, together with all the Lord's holy people, to grasp how wide and long and high and deep is the love of Christ, and to know this love that surpasses knowledge— that you may be filled to the measure of all the fullness of God. (Ephesians 3:16-19)

In this passage, Paul prayed that the Ephesians would grasp the vastness of the God of love and be rooted and established in love. God is inviting us to take on his character, which is self-sacrificial, other-oriented, and a choice-based love. I've always known that love was important—I quote it multiple times when officiating weddings—but I never connected discipleship with growth in my capacity to love God and others.

If this is the case, and I believe it is, then all that we do under the label of "discipleship" or "spiritual formation" is about growing in our capacity to be like Jesus in his love. However, it's at this level of relationship training that we must go deeper within to discover the wounds that hinder us from experiencing and giving love. This is a journey from what Henri Nouwen called the house of fear into the house of love.[4] Here we discover the roots that lie behind the fear and keep us bound up within ourselves and hinder us from risking love.[5]

If you are learning to play a musical instrument, it is helpful to have a teacher who will teach you how to develop the skills for the kind of music that you are practicing. This is where this level of training is critical. Those who are seeking to move beyond the normal group experience need a missional music teacher, someone who can "coach" them in the ways of love. Someone or something outside the group may be required to help this group process how they are growing in love with one another.[6]

Level 4: Missional engagement

This final level of relating is where I wish we could all begin! For some communities it will be. They have developed good relational skills on the first three levels and are fully ready to engage their neighbors, friends, family members, and a coworkers in missional dialogue. Notice I'm not categorizing this level as evangelism training or social ministry training. This is training in the art of dialogue, listening, and maintaining a graceful presence with others in our circles of life.[7]

The key to healthy engagement that creates life-change is dialogue. This relates to the importance of helping people answer their questions (Chapter 9).

Groups that are on mission are not going out with ready-made answers or grand plans for social change. Instead, they are engaging people in honest conversations, seeking to hear others, then returning to a conversation and sharing their lives in response. Through dialogue, they discover what God is up to and then through the *process* they see how God wants to provide life and ministry in that context.[8]

a sense of urgency

I'd like to close this chapter with a bit of hard-core honesty. For those who know me, they might find it comical that I devote so much ink to the need for relationship training because I'm not an overly relational person. I'm an introvert who loves to create, read, and think in privacy. In addition, I'm a blunt Texan who too often blurts out his opinions even if they're not welcome or invited. I find it quite comical that this is my fifth book on small group relationships when the fact is that relationships and community is hard work for me. The fact that I have to work hard at relationships helps me think through why Americans in general are not that good at them.

My prayer is that we will develop a sense of urgency to learn about relating well. Because I know that I need to learn about relating well and work harder at it because of my personality, I feel that something more significant is at stake. I want to have a good marriage and have good relationships with my four kids. I want to be a good friend and express love to others. I want to be known as a person who demonstrates love as a leader and in my community.

I rarely find people who know much about their own relational deficiencies. And while few are as introverted as I am, I've found that most of us have other things that make relating a challenge. If this is going to change, and we are going to develop community that actually makes a difference in the world, then we need to take a big dose of reality and see our relationships for what they are. Until we do that, nothing will change.

Imagine that you are that historian from 200 years in the future. What words would you use to describe how people live in your city or town? Now what words would you use to describe how people live in your church? Write those on the next page.

What words would you use to describe how people in your city or town do relationships? Now think about that same question for the people in your church. Write these words down. The goal of this exercise is not to fix things. Simply reflect honestly and become aware of the current reality. Often we try to fix things too quickly when God only wants us to see what he sees.

missiorelate
An experience with others and God
that makes a difference in the world

empower elders

did not plan to write this chapter. It's part of the accidental nature of this book. In my first outline of the book, I included it, but when writing the initial drafts I decided against it, but I'm not exactly sure why. OK, I do know . . . I was tired of writing at that point and chose a much easier option. But after reading feedback from my editor after a revision, I realized that there was a huge hole in the book concerning a crucial area. So I wrote this chapter last and placed it here. I hope you see the importance of it when you're done.

From the embryonic days of small group ministry, leadership oversight and coaching has been a crucial component. Every small group resource on my shelf speaks to the importance of establishing oversight structures. Even the house church movement sees the need for oversight. I'm not going to get into the details of these structural patterns, as I have done that elsewhere.[1] Instead, in this chapter I want to talk about what group members and groups—not just leaders—actually need in order to move into a new way of life. In a nutshell, they need elders.

how does an elder differ from a coach?

One of the common responses to my previous writings regarding this topic is,

"My group leaders don't want the input of a coach or a pastor. They find the extra meetings a waste of time. They lead groups quite well on their own." Research states just the opposite. A study has been performed on what impacts group health and life and the evidence is beyond conclusive: The single thing that positively impacts group life more than any other is the ministry of the coach.[2] So if people don't want it, just what is it that they don't want? And if it has such a huge impact, what part of coaching makes the difference?

Leaders don't want oversight. They don't want a big brother telling them what to do. And they don't want extra meetings to explain lots of theory about what *should* be happening in their small group. Some leaders want a relationship with a leader who can mentor them and encourage them on the journey, but not all leaders desire this.

But there is something that impacts groups far more than conventional coaching. Groups move forward toward MissioRelate by being "eldered." Previously, the small group world has emphasized the relationship between the coach or pastor with the leader, urging coaches to meet with leaders to support, encourage, and mentor them. And while I am in no way saying that this function needs to be discarded, as many leaders need to be coached and mentored, I am saying that MissioRelate groups need something different.[3]

Eldering might very well involve coaching and encouraging the leader, but the role of coaching does not involve the ministry of an elder. The elder invests in the people that belong to the various groups under his care. I hope you clearly understand the distinction I am making here. The common imagination of a coach—at least in the most popular books on the topic—is that the ministry is to and through the small group leaders. I am using the word elder to point to the role of a leader who cares for the groups as a whole, not just the leaders.

so what is an elder?

The term elder has been used in many different ways in the history of the church. Some traditions have a board of elders. Some talk about a teaching elder. These are official roles within established structures. Still others speak of elders as those who should be respected for their life-long commitment and walk of faithfulness in the church. Let's look at a few ways that the Bible talks about elders.

At daybreak they entered the temple courts, as they had been told, and began to teach the people. When the high priest and his associates arrived, they called together the Sanhedrin—the full assembly of the elders of Israel—and sent to the jail for the apostles (Acts 5:21).

So they stirred up the people and the elders and the teachers of the law. They seized Stephen and brought him before the Sanhedrin (Acts 5:12).

Paul and Barnabas appointed elders for them in each church and, with prayer and fasting, committed them to the Lord, in whom they had put their trust. (Acts 14:23).

This brought Paul and Barnabas into sharp dispute and debate with them. So Paul and Barnabas were appointed, along with some other believers, to go up to Jerusalem to see the apostles and elders about this question (Acts 15:2).

Do not neglect your gift, which was given you through prophecy when the body of elders laid their hands on you (1 Timothy 4:14).

The elders who direct the affairs of the church well are worthy of double honor, especially those whose work is preaching and teaching (1 Timothy 5:17).

Basically, the term for elder (*presbutas*) denotes someone who is older and more experienced. It was a common practice in the wider culture for elders to serve the Jewish religion or a city. This practice was carried over into the church. Paul established churches, then appointed elders to lead the church when he left.

The New Testament does not provide us with detailed descriptions about how the leadership of the early church was structured. It is not possible to base modern church leadership upon the specific structures of the early church because we lack a clear outline of what that looked like. I'm not using the word *elder* here to try to get back to an early church perspective. Instead, I use it to demonstrate the desperate need within the church for experienced people to guide and lead others. Age is one contributing factor, but experience in walking with the Lord is even more important. Elders have been shaped to be people who can guide others.

Eldership with this understanding will include coaching and mentoring of small group leaders, but it also means the care of and investment in the life of the small groups or house churches. I've heard it said many times that the coach should not step in and involve himself or herself intrusively in the life of a group. Instead, they should work through the leaders. The same is said about pastors. They should not visit a group because they will step on the authority of the group leader. On one level, this is good advice. Those in official church positions can exert their authority in ways that shut down other leaders. At the same time, when someone is living in a mature, whole walk with Christ and they are serving the church in leadership, why would we restrain them from ministering to the entire group? That just does not make sense. To do this in a healthy way, one that does not try to take over, we need to modify our view of leadership. I believe the following will be helpful to that end.

how do elders lead?

It is common to talk about leadership by viewing it through a vertical lens. Leaders exert power or authority through top-down approach or through a bottom-up approach. Organizational charts illustrate this with a triangle, putting the most influential leaders at the top of the top corner of the triangle for traditionally structured churches. For those who want a more organic, flat organization, the triangle is turned upside down with the key leaders being viewed underneath the rest of those they lead.

The problem with both of these leadership images is that they are static. In both situations, leadership focuses on managing people and getting them to do something for the leader. I think there is another image that works much better. We need to turn the organizational triangle on its side to show that leaders are those who set the standard for the life of MissioRelate and lead with their lives, not with their administrative abilities. The job of Christian leaders goes far beyond telling people what to do with authority or even coming under others and serving them. Leaders go ahead of the masses and clear a path for them. The illustration below demonstrates a typical organizational pyramid turned on its side to depict motion toward a vision. In it, there are four roles that are often found in churches of all kinds and sizes, filled by people who are leading with their lives as they move out ahead.

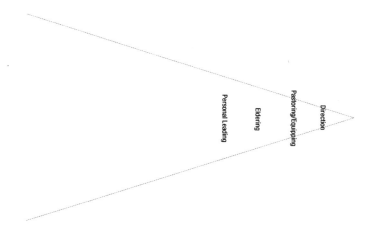

Elders lead out of who they are, not what they do. Human nature urges us to fill organizational charts by recruiting people to lead, coach, and even to fill pastoral duties and then train them for the role or position. We do it because our small group structure mandates it.

Instead, we need to empower elders, or those who lead from their current values and lifestyle. This sets a standard for a way of mission. I think this is what Jesus meant when he contrasted his kind of leadership with that of the world:

> Jesus called them together and said, "You know that the rulers of the Gentiles lord it over them, and their high officials exercise authority over them. Not so with you. Instead, whoever wants to become great among you must be your servant, and whoever wants to be first must be your slave—just as the Son of Man did not come to be served, but to serve, and to give his life as a ransom for many" (Matthew 20:25-28).

Servanthood is not about remaining busy or doing something. It is about being someone. If we think in terms of *doing* leadership, we will always get caught in the trap of trying to have the right kind of power ("over" power where we attempt to make something happen or "under" power where we attempt to support people). The problem with both approaches is that someone is in control. With "over" power, the leader is in control. When we come under people, they gain the control. Jesus did not force his will on people, but neither did he allow people to control him. Instead, he walked before them as a servant and invited them to follow.

Eldership is not about position or even age. It's not about making decisions or trying to get the organization to line up in the right direction. It's about being leaders who are willing to walk in the path of MissioRelate and show people that path.

what do elders do?

With this understanding of leadership, I want to propose that the elders are those leaders in the church who invest in, care for, and lead people into mission. The small group leader can certainly help with this goal, but elders are those with the life experience and spiritual maturity who can walk ahead and lead. The clearest instruction from the Scriptures on this comes from the hand of Peter:

> To the elders among you, I appeal as a fellow elder and a witness of Christ's sufferings who also will share in the glory to be revealed: Be shepherds of God's flock that is under your care, watching over them—not because you must, but because you are willing, as God wants you to be; not pursuing dishonest gain, but eager to serve; not lording it over those entrusted to you, but being examples to the flock. And when the Chief Shepherd appears, you will receive the crown of glory that will never fade away (1 Peter 5:1-4).

When applying this to missional small group development, elders might be the leaders of a house church of 20-50 people with small group leaders within the house church. They might oversee three to five small groups and lead periodic gatherings or help those small groups network and work together in mission.

how are elders shaped?

In some ways, elders are shaped by time, but the passing of time alone does not always produce an elder that lives out MissioRelate. If time were all we needed, then the aging of the church alone would have resulted in incredible acts of mission. Time is needed because life experience is crucial, but it's what a person does or has done with that time that shaped him or her for eldering.

Elders are shaped by public practices of leadership and the personal practices of devotion. In his excellent book *The Leadership Ellipse*, Robert Fryling writes:

> Spiritual leadership can be understood as an ellipse. One focal point is our inner spiritual life, our longings, our affections, and our allegiance to God. The other focal point is our outer world and organizational life, what we do and how we do it. Together these focal points define and ellipse that circumscribes our true spiritual leadership. It represents the dynamic tension between our soul and our actions, and gives us a mental image for personal, spiritual and professional integrity in who we are and how we lead.[4]

These two focal points aim to transform leaders from the inside out and from the outside in so that what leaders do really reflects who they are. They lead from their being as they walk out in front of others on the journey. To progress along this trajectory, there are specific practices that leaders must put into action that develop both their inner world and their outward habits. This is exactly what Fryling provides in his book and the following chapter also highlights.

The writers of *Missional Church* make a similar point about leadership, even though it is not directly tied to "eldering." This is where I got the idea to turn the organizational structure on its side. They also point out that the leaders (whether small group leaders, house church leaders or elders who oversee them) participate in a leadership community.[5] On the following page you will find the first build on the original diagram, showing how the various leadership roles create a leadership community.

This community would be formed of leaders, both novices and the experienced who are committed to practice a set of disciplines that form both their inner and their outer worlds. Here, there might be more technical training involved like how to lead a small group, pastoral skills, or basic theology. But the development of elders occurs as leaders mature by practicing the disciplines of the faith that shapes them to be the leaders that people need and actually want.

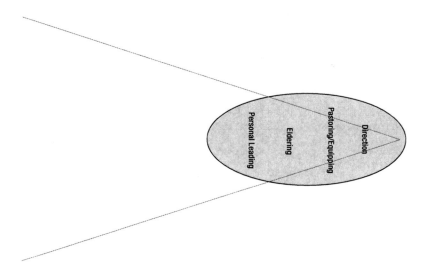

Let me close this chapter with this: A variety of small group models will work to close the back door on a church by producing groups that live out a normal life. Those models depend upon leaders who are competent to lead a group and care for the people. But to go missional depends upon elders, those who can lead others into an alternative way of living. If you miss this point and try to find the answer in a new approach, new group size, or a new fad then you will spin your wheels producing normal groups. There are a lot of ideas circulating promoting some kind of new angle, but the reality is that a move into missional is based in this very old and might I add "tested" approach. Develop elders and they will find God's path toward mission.

On the next couple of pages reflect on this chapter. In what ways does this view of eldering differ from that often seen in church structures? How is this different than coaching small group leaders? What might it look like to develop elders in your church culture? Then reflect on this question: Are you willing to invest the time and energy in such people?

missiorelate
*An experience with others and God
that makes a difference in the world*

practice your way into mission

Missional life in the kingdom of God is about living in a way that aligns with the life that Jesus demonstrated when he walked on earth. He came not only to save us from the penalty of sin. He also opened a door of freedom so that we might freely live in a new and different way. The Apostle Paul called Jesus the "new Adam," which means that he is the initiator of a new heritage or life.

This new way is a revolt against the "principalities and powers of this world" that do not line up with God's ways. They include patterns of this world such as individualism, nationalism, sexism, and racism, just to name a few. These are ingrained patterns that shape our thinking and are so common that they go unnoticed. To be transformed by the renewing of our minds (Romans 12:2) means that we must revolt against these patterns. We are revolutionaries, those who stand against the norm and offer an alternative pattern.[*]

how then should we revolt to bring about lasting transformational change?

I believe that we must practice our way into mission. That is, we must develop patterns of life that might not produce missional results in the short term, but when consistently practiced over time, the accumulative effect is one that is missional.

What does not work

Let me start by sharing how I do *not* think it happens. Turning to catchy sound bites, radical vision statements, and calls to commitment do not work. Through the years, church leaders have first established structures to mobilize people (house churches, small groups, or other organic structures) and then we stand before those same people and attempt to motivate them to get involved. We depend upon information, innovation, and motivation, expecting people to quickly line up with God's kingdom perspective. This approach yields two lackluster results: Surface change and hurt.

Surface change that lacks deep transformation

It gets people involved and often looks like success because people are mobilized to accomplish certain tasks. We point to numbers of people involved to indicate our program's success and beam with a strong, yet hollow sense of accomplishment. Recently, I read a Twitter post by a pastor bragging about the number of people who had served in short-term missions from his church. Is this a genuine measure of transformation? Is this what it means to be a Christ follower?

This tweet revealed a numeric yardstick, but I don't see where such a benchmark actually lines up with deep change in our lives. It's measurable and reportable and looks good on paper. It also has the ability to get people excited about involvement, but it only examines and measures surface change. In effect, measuring success by numbers of involved people only waters down a revolution to basic program involvement. The rest of their lives might line up with the patterns of this world, but their church involvement looks revolutionary.

Hurt that results from forced change

There is also another result that comes with radical visions and new structures designed to get people on board with the revolution. People get hurt because they are being forced to change instead of being led into embracing the change. They are told that this is *the* new form for the revolution. They are fed information and logic about why this new form is the right form and then told to go do it. Many join in, but their lives are too steeped in the patterns of this world for them to understand what the revolution is all about. They go through the motions which undermines the transformational experience of the revolution because they lack passion.

effectively communicating a deliberate revolution

There is another way of generating a revolution. Let me call it "deliberate revolution." In reality this is an oxymoron because by definition, revolutions are radical and traumatic. In the course of history, revolutions have come in many different forms, but when we commonly think about something being revolutionary, we imagine something radical, huge and led by someone with great vision. They depend upon a charismatic figure who fights to carry out the ideals of a vision and runs over whomever is in the way, all in the name of those ideals.

The goal of a kingdom revolution is a way of love. And to lead a revolution in the pattern in any other way than love will undermine the goal of love. Therefore, this revolution cannot be forced. It must be deliberate, which means that it must be generated in such a way that the people involved gain a basic understanding of what it means to be a revolutionary and then take ownership and take it on as their identity. This means that love must be both the "end" and the "means" for this revolution.

What we are called to do as God's people goes way beyond the development of a cohesive strategy to get people involved in a missional small group program. The kingdom calls for a revolution of our lives. Adding a new structure, a clear vision statement, or radical mantra has no power to instill mission within our people. Instead, we must think deliberately. What exactly does this mean?

1. Instead of centering the revolution around a charismatic hero who gears people up to enter the vision, we need to think in terms of a core group of leaders who are working together to figure out the future.[1]

2. Be patient. Deliberate revolutions develop slowly because we have to wait upon a core group to "get it." This means they start to live it out, not just gather information about it in their heads.

3. Identify a charismatic voice and take advantage of his or her ability to rally people around a key message shared in larger venues. Use this momentum gained in the larger venues[2] to move people toward participation in various ways that will help them embrace the revolution.

4. Repetition is crucial. Don't try to communicate everything about the revolution to the larger crowd. Keep the revolution message simple and broad based.

5. Use multiple media outlets for communicating the meaning of the revolution. Beyond sermons, employ blogs, vlogs (video blogs), booklets, and online forums to explain the nature of this revolution in understandable terms.[3]

In summary, when we think about a deliberate revolution, we must develop processes where we can discover together what our future looks like. If we want to create ownership, commitment, and a way of life that fits new structures, we must think in terms of processes toward a new future and not just a structure to implement a vision.

activating a deliberate revolution

When I hear the word *revolution*, I think about radical action, bold declarations, and great faith. These are the things one can write or preach about. Radical acts like these make for good stories like a person quitting his six-figure job to work with immigrants in the inner city. Or someone like Jackie Pullinger, who dedicated her life to minister to drug addicts in the worst parts of Hong Kong. Or Shane Claibourne, who casts the vision of ordinary radicals who are making major sacrifices to minster in the inner city of Philadelphia. These people are forerunners of a missional revolution.

Here's another story to illustrate a great act. In *After You Believe*, N.T. Wright shares a heroic act from a common life. On January 15, 2009, an act of greatness was reported by news agencies around the world. Captain Charley Sullenberger III safely crash-landed an Airbus A320 in the Hudson River and every passenger survived. After taking off from LaGuardia Airport, a flock of geese moved into the flight pattern and the engines shut down. To land the plane safely, all kinds of things had to happen. Wright records them:

> In the two or three minutes they had before landing, Sullenberger and his copilot had to do the following vital things (along with plenty of other tasks that we amateurs wouldn't understand). They had to shut down the engines. They had to set the right speed so that the plane could glide as long as possible without power. (Fortunately, Sullenberger is also a gliding instructor.) They had to get the nose of the plane down to maintain speed. They had to disconnect the autopilot and override the flight management system. They had to activate the 'ditch' system, which seals vents and valves, to make the plane waterproof once it hit the water. Most important of all, they had to fly and then glide the plane in a fast left-hand turn so that it could come down facing south, going with the flow of the river. And—having already turned off the engines—they had to do this using only the battery-operated systems and the emergency generator. They had to straighten the plane up from the tilt of the sharp-left turn so that, on landing, the plane would be exactly level from side to side. Finally, they had to get the nose back up again, but not too far up, and land straight and flat on the water.[4]

What Sullenberger did that day was nothing short of a miracle. Immediately he was called a hero, a wonder, and an example of greatness. This amazing act is similar to the great acts of missional action. The way that Sullenberger developed the skills needed to deal with this emergency is the same way we must develop the skills for a missional revolution. He did not merely develop these skills because he wanted them or because the time demanded them. He, along with the thousands of pilots that fly us around the world, practice such emergency situations routinely. In flight simulators, they have trained their minds to react quickly—usually failing quite a few times before they get it right—so that when an emergency happens they can respond correctly and avoid disaster.

Over the last two decades, scientists have discovered new things about the function and processes of the human brain. The parts of our brains that get worked the most actually allow a person to get more proficient at a specific task, which comes as no surprise. For example, if you want to learn a new language, practicing that language actually develops and strengths parts of the brain that would have been otherwise undeveloped.

Transfer this thought to the actions and reactions of the typical person in our churches. Responding to situations in a good, biblical or missional manner is not something that comes naturally. It is something that is practiced. Wright, along with the moral philosophers from Aristotle to Stanley Hauerwas, refer to this practiced moral response as "virtue." Wright states, "Virtue, in this strict sense, is what happens when someone has made a thousand small choices, requiring effort and concentration, to do something which is good and right but which doesn't 'come naturally'—and then, on the thousand and first time, when it really matters, they find that they do what's required 'automatically' as we say."[5]

Much of what is being promoted as missional today is equivalent to a first year pilot landing an airliner. It calls novices to jump into mission as if no practice is required. In my experience, this is an approach that produces far more failure than success.

What does *work*

I'd like to propose an alternative. Instead of jumping blindly into visible acts of mission, we should practice our way into mission. We need to develop our minds so that we have new and natural skills for missional living. Here is the challenge: most of what we need to practice for the missional life happens in unseen ways.

This is a far different approach from organizing events to do something for the community or networking with organizations that need volunteers. These activities alone might make an impact or leave an impression upon the people who invested in it, but rarely have I seen them result in missional living. One reason that it fails is that it tries to change people from the outside. And once the outward stimulus is removed, people return to the patterns of life that have shaped their inner unseen world all along. Something must be added to make these experiences life-changing.

Alongside any external outreach events, programs, or initiatives, we must equip people in the basic disciplines that generate maturity in Christ. Mission and maturity go hand in hand. The way to grow in both is to help people develop life disciplines or life rhythms that naturally produce missional action. In this way, mission will flow out of who we are, not simply what we do.

missional disciplines

Over the last few years, the importance of spiritual disciplines has resurged. No longer is it something that one or two writers like Dallas Willard and Richard Foster are promoting. We now have enough resources at our disposal to equip people in the disciplines. Now the ball is in our court. We must train our people in the disciplines in ways that fit our people and culture. In other words, when one considers his context, the way the disciplines are practiced will vary. There is no universal approach. In fact, I've found it helpful to identify a few disciplines that best fit my context and train everyone in these first with a sort of "path of least resistance" approach. On the following page, you will find a few things to teach people as they embark upon a process of developing spiritual disciplines.

1. *Create an "easy-in" starting point.* When novices to this topic are first exposed to all of the options, they become overwhelmed. It's crucial to help people start with only one or two disciplines and add more disciplines later.

2. *Be intentional.* Because of the way our brains work whenever we are trying to learn something new, we must focus on a new task in unnatural ways. It will feel like work, but that is the only way new habits will be developed is to be intentional.

3. *Focus on repetition.* The key to impacting our world (missional living) is not found in the big, visible actions, but in doing little things quietly and repeatedly. Glory is found in one-time sacrificial acts and is fleeting; *Transformation* comes when we love others in many small, seemingly insignificant ways.

4. *Do it alone.* There are some disciplines that are private and empower us to clearly hear God's voice. Without these, we will turn our walk with God into externally focused actions. There are many great resources that can help with this, including *Sacred Rhythms* by Ruth Haley Barton, *Celebration of Discipline* by Richard Foster, *The Life You've Always Wanted* by John Ortberg, *The Good and Beautiful Life* by James Bryan Smith and *Practicing Our Faith* by Dorothy C. Bass. One of the best and most challenging is Henri Nouwen's *Spiritual Formation: Following the Movements of the Spirit.* Find a resource that works for your church and begin to help people develop these disciplines.

5. *Do it with others.* Many of the spiritual disciplines cannot be practiced privately. We have to practice these with others.[6] Learn which ones are individual and which ones should be done with small group members and integrate both. Missional small groups are comprised of people who commit to practices together that change the world as they live love. (See Appendix D.)

A missional revolution—one that sticks anyway—is never started quickly. No revolution in history has ever been characterized as a sprint. Practicing our way into missional living is a long term approach. You can still organize outreach or service opportunities along the way to help get things going in that direction. Just remember we are not in the business of organizing service opportunities alone. We are in the business of providing experiences and disciplines that shape consumers into missional believers. As we do so, love is established. Our groups are not just doing something that looks missional. We become missional as love is established within us.

The impact on the world might not be a splash that can be written up in the local newspaper—if that happens it's OK but that's not the goal. Most of the time, our way of being missional is developed as we practice small acts of love repetitively. As we do this, what seems like small stuff turns into something significant.

On the next couple of pages, reflect on the current practices that are common in your church and/or groups. What is already going on that people practice that establishes them in ways of love? Now reflect on the common practices of the people in your church that get in the way of being love. Don't try to fix this or analyze it. Just see what's going on and write it down.

missiorelate
An experience with others and God
that makes a difference in the world

embrace the mystery

Mystery. Most leaders don't think about this unless of course we are watching "Murder She Wrote" or "Columbo" reruns on late night cable. We certainly don't connect mystery with what we do in shepherding people toward the kingdom. Leadership books sell well because they are written by confident leaders who clearly communicate leadership principles. If they were to highlight mystery, their books would not sell well.

We prefer to think about those things that we can control, implementing ideas we know will produce results. When we pick up a book or attend a seminar on how to improve small groups, we want to learn from someone who has a proven track record. The same is true of missional small groups or missional communities.

missional small group development is different

There is a mysterious, unknowable part to what we are trying to do. To deny this is to ignore our experience, but we have been taught to ignore this experience for a long time. We inherited an idea from church growth theory that mystery is just a lack of knowledge and it can easily be addressed and eliminated. So we analyze what works in one church and implement it in other places. Over the last 25 years, there has been so much of this happening with small groups strategies that it turns my stomach. Now churches and authors are doing it with missional living.

My friend Mark Priddy leads a community in Boise, ID that operates a coffee house. He told me that numerous church leaders have traveled to Boise to observe the various ways that people connect at the coffee house, develop community, and enjoy conversations about life and God. Inevitably, they leave thinking that they can start a coffee house in part of their church building and enjoy the same results.

Strategies work or don't work for a lot of different reasons and many cannot be fully articulated. We all know leaders who were effective in one setting but total failures in another with the same strategy. What would the mystery ratio be in a church situation? I'm not sure. One could be a better communicator than Rick Warren, a better leader than Bill Hybels, more creative than Eugene Peterson, more committed to prayer than Jim Cymbala, and have the character of Billy Graham but never see the success or effectiveness of these great leaders. Why might this be the case? We all know it's based on experiences, but do we really think through the sources of the mystery?

Groups that experience MissioRelate are no different. There is no magic formula for producing missional stories. If we don't embrace this, we will remain squarely within the normal group stories of Personal Improvement and Lifestyle Adjustment. To move beyond the normal, we must embrace the mystery rather than trying to control it.

what makes for mystery

I've often speculated how much our effectiveness in entering God's mission and living out the stories of MissioRelate depends upon mysterious factors that we cannot fully control. I'm not sure but it seems to me that mystery plays a very large part in what we do.

This does not mean that we can't do things to move in the right direction. Of course we can. Nor does it mean that we are totally out of control. Of course we aren't. But our tendency is to emphasize what we can do and how we can control things at the exclusion of the mystery. Even as I write this, there is something within me that resists what I'm writing. If I am honest, I want to be the kind of leader who controls things so that I can produce the results I want. But I know that there are other things that hinder this. Here are a few that I have observed:

Spiritual warfare is real.

This is an invisible war that permeates the entire process. We can implement all of the right elements to move people into mission, but if we miss spiritual warfare, none of them will work. Imagine a haze that infiltrates everything you do to lead people into MissioRelate and it grows darker and heavier the more people are released into God's mission. If we don't see this haze, we will remain under its control and fail to do things to combat it.

There is someone called Satan.

You might think that I am simply stating the obvious because you have read the Gospels a few times. It's hard to get around the fact that Jesus confronted evil in embodied forms of demons and Satan himself. Jesus fought against evil in a way that demonstrates that our world is caught in the middle between God's love and Satan's lies. The apostle Paul speaks about this in terms of "principalities and powers" of the universe who shape the way we do life, the patterns of our thinking, and the systems of relating to others.

Satan and his minions love it when we deny or minimize their existence. When you go to a church in Africa and people make a first-time commitment to Christ, there are often manifestations of demonic possession that make it clear a spiritual war exists. Most of us in the West don't encounter such manifestations. Instead, the lies of Satan are revealed in much more subtle ways—ways that have become so commonplace to the Western way of life that it just seems normal. Think about ways that small groups have been undercut because people started rumors about fellow members or they cast judgment on other group members because of personal struggles. Disunity, lack of trust, and an unwillingness to work through relational difficulties are all ways that Satan uses to disempower churches.

There is something called spiritual strongholds.

You might not call it by this title, but you have experienced it. You've known people who are entrapped by "strongholds in their minds" that keep them in bondage. These could be rooted in unforgiveness toward someone from the past, or believing a lie that an authority figure told them when they were a child. I remember a lady in our church sharing how one of her elementary teachers told her that she was not able to learn and wouldn't amount to anything. She carried this lie around for over forty years. It wasn't until she acknowledged it as a lie and chose to believe the truth that she was released to move out into God's call on her life.

Many churches have developed freedom encounters to help people recognize the false beliefs that entrap them. There are many excellent resources on this topic including *Encounter God* by Jim Egli and *The Bondage Breaker* by Neil Anderson. Experience has demonstrated that going through an intensive process like those suggested by these two authors helps people of all kinds see hidden strongholds. This leads to confession and acceptance of truth or repentance. The key to success here is that everyone goes through the freedom encounter as a spiritual discipline, not just those who are obviously in need.

There is something called life.

Life today is not easy. We are too busy, most people are stressed with commitments at work and in their personal lives, and in times of recession the stress only increases. Admittedly, many of us bring this stress on ourselves. For the most part, this way of life is simply the way things are done. When a church stands for an alternative way of living, the normal situations of life accelerate to fight the shift. Key leaders are transferred to another state by their corporate bosses. An elder's wife has a debilitating accident and he is forced to step down from his role to care for her. Babies are born and those who had extra time to volunteer for the church are no longer available. Of course, these life situations are endless. We can try to fight against them, but how do you fight against something that is absolutely out of your control? As long as we are alive, life will happen and a big part of this life is comprised of unanticipated change.

There is something called context.

Remember that tweet I shared earlier? "If a church is not growing, 99% of the reasons for it are internal." I'd never share that thought to pastors and missionaries in Spain or France where there is very little to no openness to the Gospel. To use the Parable of the Soils to illustrate this, they are farmers in very hard soil that will not receive the seed of the gospel, but still commanded to sow seed there.

I was raised in what used to be a little Texas town called Frisco. When I graduated from High School in 1988, it had a population of about 3800. Now it's 120,000 people and continues to grow. All over the North Dallas area you will find towns like this that grew very quickly. You will also find churches that were planted 10 to 15 years ago that are now huge. Can you determine that these churches are effective and growing because of excellent leadership? Or should their growth be attributed to their context, which is characterized by a flood of new people moving into their area looking for the kind of church that they provide? Probably both.

It's absurd to think that pastors travel to Frisco, Texas to learn about rapid church growth and return home to duplicate what they saw. What if you are a pastor in Abilene, Texas which is not seeing a lot of new growth? It's an established city and not experiencing suburban sprawl. What if you are pastoring in an economically depressed area? What if you are serving people in a rural area, primarily made up of farmers and blue color workers? Context is everything. To overlook it will mean that you miss the very mystery into which God is calling you.

There are things called traditions.

I used to think traditions were the enemy of progress. In my former way of seeing things, anyone who loved their church traditions was set against what

God wanted for the future of the church. And when you look across the church landscape, it seems that the most effective churches don't pay much attention to traditions, which only serve to slow down progress.

There is a difference between loving our traditions and being stuck in traditionalism. Traditions give us roots. They teach us patterns of worship, of relating to God, and of loving one another. People need traditions because they shape us for a way of life.

Traditionalism is different. It means that the roots of traditions have died. Instead of providing life and shaping us for worship, God and others, traditions exits because they have always done so. But while we might despise the death of traditionalism, we must not assume that we can cast aside traditions.

Healthy traditions might mean that we don't move as fast as some would like and that we don't adopt the latest church growth gimmick. Instead, traditions may be the very things that God wants to work through to achieve MissioRelate.

There is such a thing as patience.

When I read the stories of Abraham, Isaac, Jacob, and the Patriarchs, one question returns to me almost every time. Why did it take so long? God created his people by calling one family. When Abraham died, there were not many people worshipping with him. In addition, the one person who did go with him (his nephew Lot) parted ways and found himself surrounded by sin. If a church planter were to experience this today, he would shut down the church and walk away. Even when we jump forward to the end of the Pentateuch, it just seems that it took God a long time because the people he chose didn't understand that they were his representatives in the world.

Of course, all of this is pointing forward to the coming of the Messiah, but it seems to me that part took a long time also. After the Old Testament writings ended, there was 400 years of silence. 400 years? Are you kidding me? What's up with that? That's a long time!

I used to think that small groups were a great means for rapid church growth. Scripture teaches us something different: God is always in a hurry to love but he is never in a hurry to make the church into a great spectacle. He wants to create a people who actually get it to their core and not just a people who do the right things and adopt the patterns of community because it works for their lives. God's goals take time and he has all the time he wants to accomplish his goals. From our perspective, time is short. Maybe instead of faith to trust God for results, we need faith to invest in a way of being God's people that won't be realized in this generation. It could be that what we are doing today is preparing the seedbed from which our children will harvest.

There is such a thing as prayer.

Prayer changes things. Prayer impacts the world. Prayer turns churches into vibrant missional communities. When we pray for the sake of results, we miss the mystery of prayer. Prayer is one of the least productive actions we can take when we're only results-oriented. God is not calling us to him so that we can have effective ministries. He is calling us to him so that we can be with him. We revere Mother Teresa, but by North American church growth measurements her ministry was not successful. Henri Nouwen abandoned training future pastors at Yale Divinity School to become a pastor in a community for the physically and mentally disabled. His first task there was to care for a man name Adam, who could not talk, walk, or feed himself.

What if in your time with God, he calls you to lead your church to minister to a community of unregistered migrant workers? The only way to gain their trust as an outsider would be to keep everything on the down low. No one could know about the small groups that might be meeting there. You couldn't put their names in computers to track them. You could not even blog or tweet due to fears of their deportation. Of course, growth would be impossible because deportation is inevitable. But you do it anyway because this is the kind of self-sacrificial mystery into which God frequently calls us.

There is something called love.

The Bible calls the church the bride of Christ. After 12 years of marriage I've learned that I have a lot to learn. But there is one thing that I know well.

Marriage and love are not practical. You can make more and spend less money as a single person. Then when you add kids to the equation, all practicality goes out the window. Love is not practical in any way, shape, or form.

Love is the greatest thing on earth. It's what makes the world turn.

If we take the metaphor of the church as the bride of Christ seriously, then we need to reframe how we gauge effectiveness. The way we war in this world against the enemy is through self-sacrificial love.

I am reminded of some of the stories that Ralph Neighbour used to tell about his experimental church in the 1970s in west Houston. The stories of a vice president of an oil company who was part of a group that supported the work of a house where people dried out from drugs. Stories of groups that ran an English as a second language ministry to build relationships with Japanese housewives. Stories about a local mechanic who used his shop to mentor teens and the group that came around him to support what he did. He writes about it in his book, *The Seven Last Words of the Church*. Later he became known for helping establish cell church thinking in North America, which sadly became identified with church growth and large churches. But in his imagination, church growth was never his driving force. He was driven to find a way to equip his people and empower them for mission (even though he did not use that language.) He was seeking a way for the church to be what it was called to be. He longed for it to be the beautiful bride.

learning to be the bride of Christ

In today's tradition, at least in the West, brides prepare themselves for the wedding ceremony with four things: something old, something new, something borrowed, and something blue. As Christ's bride, the church is preparing itself for the return of the bridegroom when our union with Christ will be complete. My prayer is that the words in this book help prepare the church for that day, as we embrace the old, new, borrowed, and blue.

Something old

I've tried to be very clear in this book about the fact that there have been many forerunners who pioneered that which we now call *missional*. I have learned much from the missional prophets who were doing group life that made a difference 30 or 40 years ago and are ignored and overlooked today. Some have jumped on the missional fad and renamed traditional outreach activities. But there is a deeper truth or a deeper story that is coming to life. Being missional is not a recent fad. It is a river of life that has flowed through God's creation for a long, long time. When we recognize this old rhythm of God's life in the world, we begin to work with God and step into his river.

Something new

On the other hand, I have brought clarity to how the four stories approach to understanding small groups makes things completely new. This perspective really has changed everything for me. I can remember the day and the exact details of it when the light bulb turned on for me. I suddenly saw the four stories come to life and I have not thought about groups in the same way since. For those tired of the "small groups in a box" approach, this new approach will prove refreshing. The more widespread the stories become, the more we will see community that really does make a difference in our world.

Something borrowed

I am not ashamed to admit that I borrow ideas. Someone once said, "There is nothing new under the sun." I don't claim to have come up with this stuff in isolation. This book is only meant to put pieces together in a way that helps church leaders create environments that produce new stories. This borrowing is multifaceted in that I am not simply looking within small group material to find what kinds of groups play the rhythms that make a difference in the world. As I have taught these concepts, it has become clear that Apostle Paul, Saint Benedict, John Wesley, and Dietrich Bonhoeffer wrote similar things. I also have been shaped by those who have returned from the mission field and have helped the church in the West understand what it means to be missionaries in our own land.

Something blue

Having lived in Minnesota for five years, I have grown to appreciate a blue sky. Winter days are short, dark, and cold. But when I put on my coat on a day like today, walk out in the sub-zero weather, and look up at a blue sky, everything changes within me and I see the world differently. Hope is released and my imagination is reborn. Our hope is in Christ in us, the hope of glory. God, in Christ, through the Spirit is at work in this world, even in the various manifestations of the church that we know quite well in the West. As we allow the Spirit of God to write new stories through us, the clouds part and the hope of a blue sky changes everything.

On the next pages, write your thoughts and reactions to this chapter. Why do we put so much emphasis on strategy and structures in the American church setting? Why do we seem to ignore the reality of mystery? How have you seen mystery at work in your church in the past? What are some ways that you can create an environment that might embrace mystery and allow the Spirit of God to guide and empower the church to move forward toward MissioRelate?

a process for
changing everything

missiorelate
*An experience with others and God
that makes a difference in the world*

aim the journey at missiorelate

When flying in a larger commercial aircraft, we wouldn't walk right up to the plane and leap on to it. Instead, we must use a carefully engineered boarding process. Tickets are secured from the airline's front counter. Then we move through security, enter the concourse, and find our gate. When the crew and aircraft is ready, we walk down a jet way to enter into a vastly different experience of flying at 500 miles per hour (compared to walking around or riding in an automobile).

For most of our people, jumping straight into a MissioRelate small group would be a bit like attempting to board one of a Boeing 777's open doors without the services of the airport buildings and jet ways. If you stop to consider this stark contrast in lifestyle, MissioRelate is so different from normal church life and our life experience that the leap may never be attempted.

Experiencing the stories of Personal Improvement and Lifestyle Adjustment can be used to guide people through the concourse and prepare them to get on the plane of MissioRelate. These two stories can help people discover a life together on mission. In other words, a church can use them to prepare people to get on the missional small group airplane and take flight. Here's where the 40-day campaign is valuable, followed by semester-length groups to help people learn through experience what missional living is and move toward it. Some will catch it quickly. Others may take years to get it. But it's a great place to start with people *if we are committed to helping them move past normal stories into MissioRelate stories.*

MissioRelate must not be something we commit to in theory. Nor is it something we announce to the congregation as a new vision, expecting people to line up, sign up, and live up to the vision instantly. It is something we learn to do on our journey through life. If the people we are leading are at the very beginning stages of their own community journey, we should not denigrate them because they're unwilling to make a massive leap to where we find ourselves. As I've stated before—and will state again and again—we must lead people from where they are today, not where we believe they should be.

At the same time concourses can be dangerous places. Human nature will surely dictate the development of the latest and greatest concourse because they trick us into thinking that normal group experiences are enough. This is where most of the information on small groups fails miserably. It's not that the strategies don't work or are unnecessary. The misgiving is in the fact that these strategies short-change the journey and make the concourse the goal of it all. They stop short, aiming for good Bible studies or assimilating people into normal groups. While keeping the tension between the vision for MissioRelate and people's current realities, we must aim people to move toward MissioRelate, which requires an examination of how (or if) we are preparing people for life on mission.

Author's Note: It's time to switch gears! What you will read from this point forward is more practical and instructive versus inspirational. I wanted to make sure that this directive-styled information was not lost in lots of extra words that make for smoother reading but draw one's attention from the main point.

---

journeying through the four stories

Our path is now clear: we must lead people through one story to the next by learning new skills. These skills must effectively draw in individualists—those looking to get their consumer-driven spiritual needs met through a church program—and help them understand how to take steps from Personal Improvement all the way through to Missional Re-Creation.

In no way do I think that everyone must progressively move through all four stories in a linear fashion. People will jump into the stories at various points of entry. Just don't make the futile assumption that everyone in your church is ready for the missional experience.

Additionally, I have not made the assumption that every church must create programs to move people through these four stories. This will become obvious in Chapter 18, but let me state here that I start with the knowledge that almost every American, whether Christian or non-Christian, comes into a church experience with preconceived notions about what the church is about. Some will enter this journey through more traditional means, through a weekend worship service, while others might come to Christ in organic relational ways, through the relationships in a missional small group. In either case, no one in the modern West comes to Christ or the church with a blank slate about what it means to be a part of a church. Most have expectations about what God can do for them and what the church should do to improve their lives. Therefore, while the journey through these stories might look very different in a mega-church of 3000, a mid-sized program based church of 300, a traditional family church of 70 or a house church of 30, people will need to be directed toward a journey that points them to MissioRelate or they will remain mired in their normal church expectations that generations of cultural Christianity has taught them.

The most effective way to demonstrate this journey is to break it down to its most simple components, but this is risky. Making it overly simplistic is not truly accurate because life is not linear as the diagram on the next page implies. The following is just a way to simplify the journey that some will take through the four stories.

The Four Stories Illustrated

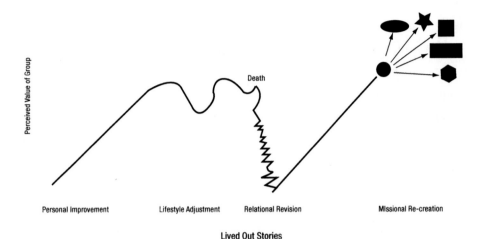

Lived Out Stories

When a person enters group life for the first time, it is often for selfish reasons. Personal improvement groups provide such experiences. Here, they'll make a few friends, learn more about the Bible, and sense God's love. This same group of individuals seeking personal improvement will no doubt experience troubled waters after just a couple of months together. After all, a group cannot continue and be called successful by the members of that group if everyone in the group is self-focused. Lifestyle Adjustment is the next natural step for people who have bonded and see the needs of others and find a desire to love them by serving or simply not being *completely* self-focused.

Look carefully at the middle of the diagram. If an individual or a group wants more than a Lifestyle Adjustment experience, a death to one's self is required. The kind of community that God is shaping cannot be piled on top of what we bring to a group to make it significant. It must start anew with a foundation of selflessness.

Let's go back to the airport analogy for a moment. There's a big difference between a concourse and the Boeing 777. If we want to fly somewhere, we must release control by trusting the pilot to fly us to our destination safely. We do this because driving across country or rowing a boat across an ocean is not an option. To move from the second to the third story we must admit that the familiar life that we know today is no longer valuable compared to the life we could be leading. Typically, this comes in the form of dying to our individualism where our faith in God is private. When we move forward from Lifestyle Adjustment to Relational Revision, we die to our "me-faith" and replace it with a "we-faith."

As groups develop the rhythms of missional group life through the adoption of various practices, they will discover that their engagement with the neighborhood directly impacts how they are shaped as a group. This is why there is no missional small group (or missional community) model to adopt, emulate, or even write about for that matter. When we practice life together in the neighborhood, the unique context for each group will have a direct impact on the form, size and shape of that group. This is the reason that the shapes in the diagram under Missional Re-creation vary. There is no one size fits all. At this point, we must remain sensitive to the context and the kinds of people in which a group is living out the Gospel. The form of the group is not critical (where the group meets, how long it meets, what it studies, and so forth) to its success. It's all about the rhythms.

When we view small group life as a journey, there is freedom for all four stories to exist within any one church. And many times all four stories will be experienced even in one small group. Much of the time this fact is missed, so pay attention here. Refuse to be the leader who is razor-focused on one way of doing groups. Radical churches focus only on missional patterns of church life, missing those who are living within the normal range. Other churches focus on small groups as a program, working overtime to assimilate people into "normal" groups at the expense of experimenting with radical groups. A MissioRelate church embraces both the normal and the radical so a shift can occur.

When presenting this concept to a group of pastors a number of months ago, a church leader from Ireland told me about a group that had been a challenge for him. He shared that they were very innovative and their creativity and zeal had resulted in some radical experiments. They regularly shared meals, sacrificially supported one another, and poured months of their time investing in the people of a specific apartment building. Before my presentation, he thought that they no longer fit the norms of the church and assumed they would spin off as a separate church. Within this new paradigm, he saw how this missional group could serve as a lived experiment out of which others could learn.

developing a process

This next diagram illustrates a process that a church can develop to help people move into MissioRelate. Let me recommend that you dog-ear this page right now for future reference. I will break apart each element of this diagram in the rest of this chapter and in the next three. This is how I suggest that leadership imagine how they move people along the path toward MissioRelate. Note that this process assumes that a church has a weekend service of some kind. And it assumes that people enter the church first through that portal. That is not always the case. When MissioRelate becomes more and more the norm, people will enter into the community of the church in all kinds of ways and relationships. But the easiest way to introduce a new idea is to start with the most common assumptions about how things work in the church and then explain other alternatives later. Other patterns of entry into these stories will be introduced in future chapters.

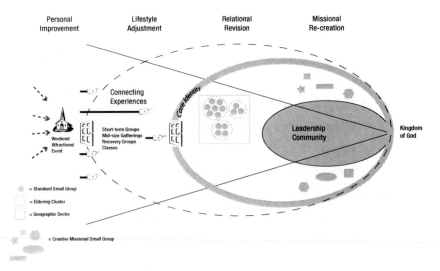

This diagram illustrates strategies for all four stories to exist side-by-side. The horizontal triangle is wider at the left end because there are more people who live out Personal Improvement. It gets smaller as you move to the right because fewer people will count the cost to move into MissioRelate life patterns. Also note that the triangle is open to the left, meaning that all are welcome to take this journey and go as far as they choose.

While there is not a one-to-one relationship between the various structures in this diagram and the four stories, there is a loose affiliation. Personal Improvement can be affiliated with the weekend services and the small group programs that are directly connected to and driven by those services, like 40-day church-wide campaigns.

The Lifesystle Adjustment story can be affiliated with various connecting strategies from semester groups, common small groups, discipleship classes, service opportunities and even affinity-based recreation groups.

Relational Revision is depicted by the small circles where small communities are intentionally working together to learn to be missional while Missional Re-creation is depicted by the small squares as they are more creative and trying to engage the context.

When established churches start moving people toward missional small groups, they need to think in terms of this diagram because they already have a weekend service and some kind of connecting strategies in place. The question is not what they should have or not have. The question is how to use what they do have to move people toward MissioRelate. In other words, most established churches have the main parts of the airport; they just need to be retooled to guide people toward the plane.

In the next three chapters, I will break down the strategies that correspond to the four structures. (For recent church plants, house churches, or organic church networks, feel free to jump ahead to chapter 18 as chapters 16 and 17 focus on systems that are part of established churches.)

Don't begin the next chapter until you've taken a moment to stop and think about the primary activities of your church's life, from the weekend service to the essential programs. List each one and name its goal by answering this question: What does this experience equip people to do next? Or, What is this specific activity moving people toward?

On the opposite page, you'll find a diagram similar to what is found on page 216, but it does not include any specific programs or church structures. Start on the left side of the diagram and begin to list the various things that your church does and fit them into the structure. Include everything from Sunday services, Wednesday night meetings, Sunday school programs, service opportunities, men's programs, women's programs, youth, children's ministry, etc. Note that most of these things will fall under the category of "Connecting Experiences." That is to be expected. The key at this point is to list what you have so that you can see what you have to build upon. Don't judge it or even evaluate it. Just look at what you have.

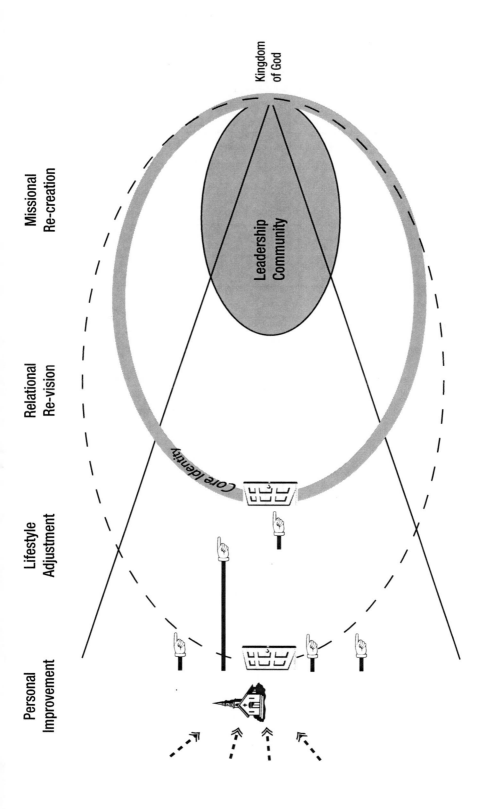

missiorelate
*An experience with others and God
that makes a difference in the world*

aim worship services at missiorelate

When we consider the vision of providing a process for moving people into missional community, we must ask: What is the role of the weekend service within this vision? Do we continue what we have been doing or is there a better way? One way to help process through these questions is to identify a few metaphors or images that are common in the church world and use these as points of contrast. These include:

A Hospital—A place where people can come and find healing and receive grace. In this context, wounded people are welcomed, messages of grace are the focus, and people are left to themselves to receive the healing that they feel they need to pursue.

A Fork in the Road—A place where people consistently hear the salvation message and are given the opportunity to pray to receive Christ as savior. Whether a seeker service or a traditional evangelical church, the primary point is to give non-believers the chance to meet Christ for the first time.

A Concert—A place where people have an engaging experience, whether through the music or through preaching, that involves the senses and emotions to provide a spiritual experience. The point is to give people a show that will effectively communicate the message and get people to return the following week.

A Nest—A place where all the people feel warm and welcomed. The focus lies on meeting their needs in a way that makes them feel comfortable and loved.[1]

A Seminar—A place where people receive sound biblical teaching. Usually in these settings, the focus lays on the unique gifts of a prominent speaker and it can be very intense and theological. (Those from Dallas Theological Seminary or the John MacArthur point of view might be found in this category.)

A Family Reunion—A place where people who know one another can connect each week and celebrate their common allegiance to Jesus. Most often this is an experience or feature of smaller churches.

I am sure that there are additional images we could identify, but these provide a broad stroke of the brush that have one thing in common: the effectiveness of each is measured according to a "boomerang effect." The Sunday service is the place of sending out for the purpose of having people return to the Sunday service. This should not be read as being harsh or judgmental because this has been the point of every form of the weekly church service in America for generations. Since the move away from the parish system of Europe toward the creation of a competitive church market, the subliminal (and sometimes not so subliminal) goal has been how to get people to fill seats.

I state this goal rather bluntly because this is the most obvious way to know if we are effective in attracting people. In addition, most of us know how to do a service that will fill seats and keep people satisfied enough to come back. If we choose to assess the role of the weekend services in our vision to move people into mission, then we must reassess the goals that we are measuring from these services.

a goal beyond the boomerang

Over the past 25 years, there have been many who have criticized the boomerang effect of the weekend services. They propose alternative images to help church leaders challenge people to see church as more than a weekly service.

A Pagan Mistake—Some argue that the weekend service is solely a product of Constantinian church life. In fact, they argue that a corporate service of more than 20 people is unbiblical. Therefore the only biblical place to do church is in homes. This view is based on a certain kind of exegesis, which causes the interpreter to apply New Testament history to other contexts in an acontextual manner. There are many factors that lent to the fact that the church met in the way it did in the first century. While many of the church patterns adopted over the centuries are mistakes rooted in paganism and some of them should be tossed, the answer is not to simply apply first century patterns in 21st century contexts without doing the hard work of thinking and praying through what contextual bodies of Christ might look like today. Nor does this mean that the large group worship is simply unbiblical because they did not practice them in the first century like we do today.

An Unnecessary Waste of Time—There is a common critique by many that corporate worship and teaching are not beneficial and therefore opt out of it completely. This image is a reaction often expressed by long-term church members who are tired of the boomerang experience and want more. The tendency is to overreact and "throw the baby out with the bath water" instead of seeing how the large group service can be re-imagined.

A Balancing Act—Many churches see the large group/small group structure as a balancing act. Weekly worship seeks to both welcome new people and charge up the troops who are engaged in group life. The assumption of this image is that all small groups will strive to be missional in nature simply because they are meeting in groups. The role of the large group is to cast vision for small group life and provide the means for getting people in them. However, most people attend church services with a certain set of expectations of what church should be. They are not equipped to participate in a missional small group. As a result, the small group experience gets watered down to a banal weekly meeting where people are nice to one another and support one another at minimal levels.

A Sorting Pen—This image is simply one of necessity. So many people are attending mega churches that the staff and lay leaders are unable to get everyone connected. They know that the big Sunday event is not enough and they may even articulate that the Sunday event is not even the main point of the life of the church. But because of the sheer numbers of people connected to the Sunday event, they attach something to the Sunday event periodically to sort people into groups, hoping to close the back door. They usually develop or purchase small group curriculum that is good enough to overcome the fact that leaders are not trained to shepherd people in groups. In fact, they don't often have leaders, calling them hosts.

an alternative image

Earlier, I suggested that moving into missional small group life is similar to flying on a commercial airplane, requiring ticketing centers and concourses that help us board and fly on a big jumbo jet. Following the analogy, the concourse that takes us to the plane are the things that a church does to intentionally equip people for missional group life. The ticketing area of an airport is

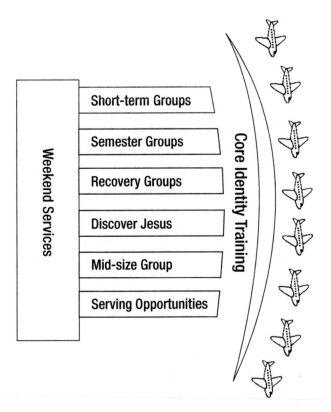

similar to the weekend services, pointing people to the various concourses that will help them become equipped for mission.

The point of the weekend service is to welcome people so that they know where to go, make it clear where they are going (where this specific airport can take them), and provide clear guidance on how to get there. All three parts are required for an effective ticketing process. If a new person to an airport does not know where to go when they get out of the car, they could very well turn around and return home. If it is not clear where a specific airport can take someone, then a person might purchase a ticket, not knowing that they want to go to a different destination. And if they don't know how to get to the airplane, they could walk around the airport indefinitely.

A church I worked with articulated the primary goals of their weekend services in this way:

1. Create a space where people feel welcomed.
   - Create a hospitable atmosphere.
   - Listen to where people are.
   - Invitr them to hear God.
   - Understand our people and know what they need to hear.

2. Provide opportunities for people to encounter God.
   - Introduce a beautiful vision of the kingdom *(for newbies)*.
   - Expand and develop awareness of and commitment to a kingdom vision *(for folks who've been around)*.
   - Create themes that point people toward the vision.
   - Confront the "idols" of our culture.
   - Encourage people; provide a "boost" to help them re-center themselves and head back into the culture.
   - Do these things through worship, prayer, and/or sermons.

3. Clearly promote and explain the next steps.
   - Point to practical pathways for being involved; create clear, simple next

steps that are chosen for the "audience" we have present.

- Recognize that the weekend is part of a whole and we therefore need not address everything.
- Inform established people of church-wide functions.
- Create awareness for events, trips, ministry needs, and ministry startups.
- Generate financial support for mission trips (fund-raisers).

In summary, this chapter looked at how we can practically reconcieve the weekend attractional services. This comprises the first part of the diagram on page 216. We have lots of experience in leading Sunday worship services under the assumption that the goal is to get people to come back to that service. In other words, we know how to do Sunday services when they are the beginning and the end of what we do. And with all the technology that we have today, we have new and endlessly creative opportunities for us to *enhance* that experience. But if we rethink the weekend service, we will move people toward new kinds of mission opportunities. The Sunday service is no longer the end. It becomes a tool for empowering people and freeing them for mission.

Of the images that are described on page 216 and 226 regarding the weekend services, which best fits the corporate services at your church? Is there another image that fits better? Are your services based on the boomerang goal? How might you change this to help people move beyond the current experience? Reflect on this on the next couple of pages before you read any further. The next chapter will look deeper at how we make the path clear by reconceiving connecting strategies so that people know how to navigate the path toward life in MissioRelate groups.

missiorelate
*An experience with others and God
that makes a difference in the world*

aim connecting experiences at missiorelate

If the weekend service is a ticket counter, then Personal Improvement and Lifestyle Adjustment groups (recovery, men's, women's, couples, short-term study, and Christian foundation classes) would be the concourses. These connecting experiences provide ways for people to move beyond the ticketing counter toward the missional story experienced on the planes.

In reality, many people will walk up and down the concourses living out the stories of Personal Improvement and Lifestyle Adjustment no matter how hard we work to get them to move toward the airplane of missional life. Every church must determine how God is leading them to minister to "concourse people." Some will be called to provide the concourses with hopes that people will eventually get it, while other churches will be far more intentional and focused on getting people to move toward missional living and therefore not provide extensive concourses. I have participated in both experiences. And there are pros and cons for both. Providing concourses that provide clear routes toward MissioRelate requires a constant balancing act because a church is required to carry out multiple things at once. Most established churches will have to do both, at least in the short-term.

In addition, it's tempting to focus on developing great connecting (concourse) experiences that keep people comfortable in their current stories. About 20 years ago, I was forced to stay overnight in the Minneapolis/Saint Paul airport on the way back from a mission trip to Russia. It was a miserable night because there was nothing to do and no place to comfortably sleep. This is not the case today. Now there are stores of all kinds to browse, restaurant options like those found in a mall, and much more comfortable seating. And in some international airports, you can even rent a sleeping room by the hour.

The average church person expects pastors and leaders to provide great connecting strategies, the kind that make us feel safe and keep us from looking for programs found in other churches. While there is nothing wrong with excellence, we must carefully make the purpose of these connecting experiences clear. Connecting is not a destination, but rather an important segment of a missional journey.

connecting experiences that work for your church

To develop a concourse plan that best fits your context, here is a process to use to foster the stories of Personal Improvement and Lifestyle Adjustment and move people beyond them.

Step 1: Articulate the purpose of "connecting small groups."
This step is meant to help leadership get clear and realistic about the expectations of these kinds of groups. This is where the four stories can help a church clarify all involved what one can expect from these kinds of groups.

Step 2: Determine "connecting experiences" that are already in place.
Honestly, not all churches need connecting groups. In many cases, people are already connected and living the story of Lifestyle Adjustment. Consider a church of 70. Social belonging is quite natural. Even in a church of 250, almost every gathering provides an opportunity for people to connect in social ways.

In addition, connecting group strategies are needed most in churches where there is a big front door. They know how to attract people through the weekend event. If a church is not attracting a good number of people through the weekend services, then the development of a new connecting strategy may not be necessary. Most likely it is already in place.

Another issue to consider is the social construction of life within a specific location. For example, if a geographic area is characterized by a relatively stable population where people do not relocate frequently, then it is likely that people already have social connections. Attempting to establish a competing connecting strategy will be met with some level of natural resistance because people are already connected in social networks.

Step 3: Don't re-create the wheel.

You don't have to figure out a connecting strategy on your own. There are numerous books on this subject. In most cases, when churches thought they were developing a missional group strategy they ended up developing a really good connecting group system. Novelty is not required. Almost any imaginable strategy has been developed and most of the good ones have been perfected. Save yourself the time and money and learn as much as you can up front from others. It will prove cheaper in the long run.

At the same time, don't maintain a "lock, stock, and barrel" attitude. No strategy will transfer from one local church set in a unique context into another in its exact form. We can learn from others, but we need not emulate another church as if the Spirit of God speaks and leads one church and does not others that choose to copy it.

When I survey the landscape of connecting group strategies there are a few that stand out:

The Ongoing Open Group Strategy - This is a very common strategy where all groups are open to receive new people and then groups multiply as new leaders are raised up from within the groups and released after training is completed. Essential for this strategy to work is the fact that all groups are open, which requires an expectation and the skills to receive new people into group life. The types of groups can vary from serving groups to deep Bible study. Key Resource: *Becoming a Church of Small Groups* and *Seven Deadly Sins of Small Group Ministry* by Bill Donahue and Russ Robinson.

The Semester Sermon Study Strategy - With this approach, all groups meet for 13-weeks, and the groups cycle over again two or three times per year. There are no permanent groups, except for those who continue from one semester to the next. The focus of all groups is to study the sermon. Key Resource: *Sticky Church* by Larry Osborne.

The Semester Multi-Option Strategy - This strategy is very similar to #2 but the difference is that groups vary in what they do or study. Usually each semester opens with some form of small group fair where leaders educate interested people in the kind of group they will form. Key Resource: *Activate* by Nelson Searcy.

The 40-day Campaign Strategy - With these groups, people sign up for a six to seven week commitment to a short-term group with no expectations that the group will continue. The group content is tied to weekly sermons, a study guide for personal reflection and some sort of activity, whether a service project or an equipping event. Key Resource: lifetogether.com, Saddleback Church, and www.markhowelllive.com.

The 9-month Closed Group Strategy - Groups in this system last from September to May and all are closed. The expectation is that a new leader will be raised up within each group to start a new group during the following September launch. The content of such groups can be sermon studies, allowing groups to choose their own or a specific discipleship program. Key Resource: *Creating Community* by Andy Stanley and Bill Willits.

The "Let's Throw People Together" Strategy - This might not sound strategic, but it actually works. Gather all those interested and form small groups that meet at the church building for four weeks. Each on-campus group is formed by the geographical location in which the member lives. Identify a host within each group who can facilitate simple questions. During the initial four weeks, the groups are led though some basic curriculum to help the members bond and to help them better understand the parameters of what it means to meet together. After four weeks they move the meetings into the host home.

The "Quick! Let's Throw People Together" Strategy - A variation of this strategy is to begin after one large group gathering meeting in the host home. In such cases the curriculum is usually video-based so the group can form around a program that carries the weight while relationships and leadership are being developed. Key Resource: Southeast Christian Church, Louisville, KY.

The Mid-sized Program Driven Strategy - With this approach, people gather around a topic or a need in a programmatically driven mid-size group and then they break out into small groups for the balance of the evening. Examples of this are recovery group programs, Alpha, spiritual formation classes, and so forth.

Step 4: Analyze the culture of your church.
The next step is to think through the cultural questions related to the people you are trying to connect. Important questions might include:

- What is the general socioeconomic level of those we seek to connect?
- What is the level of education among these people?
- How much church background do these people possess?
- What is the level of cultural uniformity within our church?

Considering most of the connecting strategies were developed by middle-class suburban churches, we can generally conclude that when the demographics of a church reflects higher answers to these four questions, the easier it will be to connect people.

When a church is more culturally diverse, including those who are in lower socioeconomic brackets or have less education and less church background, then connecting people in small groups that meet in homes will prove to be more of a challenge. A struggling single mom with four kids and two

235

jobs who makes it to church three out of four weeks a month is probably not interested in opening up her home to host a group. It matters very little how easy we make it with video curriculum. The challenge is simply too much for some. In addition, if there is significant cultural diversity, the communication skills required to connect on a social level make it a challenge to empower people quickly enough to lead groups that meet in homes.

As a result, the first seven connecting strategies seem to work better in homogenous, suburban churches comprised of people who have transferred from other churches.

Step 5: Learn about a strategy or combination of strategies.

Do you research. Learn as much as you can. Gather a team of people who are on the same page concerning what you are trying to do. Do this before you announce it or calendar anything.

Step 6: Secure commitment for the approach you have chosen.

There are a lot of right ways to do something and this holds true of connecting strategies. Most of the time, a strategy fails not because it is flawed, but because the church has not found uniform, committed buy-in to the strategy. Because most of these strategies depend upon multiple groups within a leadership system of a church working together, everyone must be committed to the success of the strategy, not just the small group team.

To summarize, this chapter explained how we can practically reconcieve connecting strategies. These comprise the second part of the diagram on page 216. Again, like the weekend services, we have a lot of experience providing these experiences for people, but we need to rethink how we do them so that they point to MissioRelate. With this new perspective, we can use our experience to move people through connecting and into mission. Some people will start off volunteering in children's ministry or ushering at worship services. As they hear a vision for mission and receive equipping to live out that mission, they can step out beyond where they began. Carefully engineered connecting experiences allow people to start where they are comfortable while being challenged to move on.

Stop here and think about your connecting strategies. What do you already have in place in your church? Which ones are the most effective? Why? How were they developed, and how well do they operate? How could they be used to point people toward MissioRelate? Which strategies in their current form cannot be used this way? How might they be changed? Use the space on the next couple of pages to reflect on these questions.

Then, work through the steps for developing a connecting strategy on pages 232-236. Write down your thoughts. The next chapter will look further at how we make the path clear so that people know how to navigate the path toward life in MissioRelate groups.

missiorelate
*An experience with others and God
that makes a difference in the world*

create a
clear path to
missiorelate

few years ago, an organizational consultant led our pastoral team through two days of teambuilding processes. It came at a critical time for us. As a team, we were not collaborating enough and we needed an outsider to introduce new ideas. I will never forget one thing she said . . .

"There are a lot of right ways to do something."

At first, I bristled when I heard this statement because I usually look for one method that everyone can implement. To be honest, to find the "right" way just feels a lot safer. Today, I have realized just how right she was. That one statement has saved me a great deal of stress and fear of failure.

There are a lot of right ways for churches to enter into MissioRelate. Your right way will depend on many factors, which we will get to below. The key is to find your right way, whatever it is, and stick with it. As I stated in the first pages of this book, the flywheel will not start turning because you found a magical formula or chose the next trend that promises miraculous success. In almost every case, your right way will only work for you in your specific situation and your specific local context. It cannot be copied from another source. But there are a few things that will help your right way work better, which I will now share with you.

communicating your right way

In this book, I have introduced ideas, concepts, diagrams, and processes that are meant for those who are pushing the flywheel. That is, this information is designed for those who are overseeing, leading, and shaping the future of your church. I have observed pastors and leaders who read books like this or attend a conference on church strategy and they start to communicate that information in the same way that they received it. That information was not written for the average person in the church. While it might address the needs of the leaders, it does not meet others where they are and communicate the "right way" clearly enough.

As you move toward MissioRelate, the key is to communicate your right way clearly and simply. While life will always be more complex than any process you develop, it is absolutely essential to present a journey toward MissioRelate that people can write down on a napkin over lunch with a friend. Make it clear. Keep it simple. Test it out with people and see if they understand where the church is going and what it means to participate in it. Then repeat it often.

Repetition might seem boring to you and other church leaders, but most people need to hear or see things in action multiple times before they are able to get their minds around an idea. Church leaders typically promote a new idea once or twice and grow frustrated because people are not jumping on board immediately. The reality is that very few people like new ideas and they will not feel comfortable with anything new until they have heard a lot about it.

Finding your right way

There are a lot of factors to consider when trying to find a path or process that works for you. I am convinced that the diagram on page 216 can be laid over any church situation, but the specific way that you do it will vary. You will need to take into account your church tradition, the context where you are set, the size of your church and the gifts that people in the church bring to the table.

Let me illustrate ways that the diagram on page 216 can be applied to specific church situations using simple language and clearly communicating a process for moving people into MissioRelate.

Example #1: A Church of 3000

I know of one church of this size that's been shaped by the speaking gifts of a lead pastor, but now they want to lead people into mission. The church has developed an extensive recovery and counseling ministry, and has numerous ways for people to get connected. However, they want to make sure that they are challenging people to move beyond relational connection. The process that they have developed looks like this:

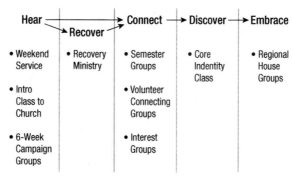

Everyone can understand this process. It is simple enough to show people the way and even converse around an important fact: while the journey is linear in some ways, in many ways it is much more complicated just as life is far more complicated than any diagram can communicate.

Example #2: A church of 250

Large churches have lots of resources (money and people) to do lots of creative things compared to smaller congregations. They have the ability to develop more concourses while at the same time developing the MissioRelate vision. In most churches, this is not a luxury. The reality of limited leadership and financial resources is an every present reality. The key in most smaller churches is to hone in on what you are called to do and then do it. Here is another approach to communicating the journey toward MissioRelate:

Envision - See what God is doing in this body and around you in our world as we gather in weekly worship and have monthly church-wide "town meetings" to converse about what we see God doing.

Envelop - Join together with a few others in a three-month group based around various topics of study.

Equip - Participate in "Equipping for Mission" classes which will prepare the person for the ministry calling that God has uniquely created him or her to do.

Engage - Discover the freedom in ministering with others through one of the mission groups that is engaging the neighborhood.

In this example, the Envelop groups would be limited in number and kind to keep leadership time resources free for the last two parts of the journey, Equip and Engage. This can prove quite difficult because in the average church, most of the energy naturally flows toward maintaining weekly services and programs. In most cases, this will not change overnight, but it is absolutely essential that pastors and key leaders find ways to change how they invest their time.

Example #3: A small organic church

When I was a part of an experimental church in the early 1990s, we had all kinds of people join our very non-traditional, organic/missional church experience (even though we did not call it either organic or missional at the time). We were doing Relational Revision at every level of our church and we had no official concourse experiences. But when people came to our church, they presumed we would fulfill normal church expectations. This was even true of those who joined who had little to no church background. Even though we did not need to establish specific structures to match the four stories like one might find in a church of 3000 or even of 250, we still needed processes to lead people through the four stories. People came to use with what we called "hidden agendas." Most of the time the individuals themselves did not even

244

know they possessed them, making them truly hidden. Our greatest challenge was that we lacked a clear way to help people see and deal with them. So they participated in the life of the church without a clear understanding why we worshipped corporately as we did, how we connected as a network of groups, and why we did not do the things that traditional churches did.

Over the years, I have found various small organic churches that do a good job of helping people walk through the four stories, even though they themselves might not use this language. I have gleaned from what they do and pulled together an example of what we should have done in our experimental church to help people get clear about the journey:

Relate - Most people begin participating in our church through a relationship. You are always free to ask as many questions about our church with anyone you meet and participate as much as you desire.

Welcome - If you want to go a little deeper, come to our monthly Welcome Conversation, which meets in the home of one of the church leaders. This is a short 90 minute meeting that gives a basic introduction to who we are as a church.

Learn - We have various ways to help you grow in your walk with Jesus. This process starts with an introductory six-week class that will help you on that journey. It is led by an excellent teacher and the format is very conversational.

Participate - While you have already been participating along the way, our goal is to help you find how God is working in and through your life so that you might more fully participate in what God is doing.

Organic churches do not need to develop all of the programs to walk people through the various stories; they can walk through those stories within the relationships in their small groups, house church meetings, and discipling relationships. But they do need a clear process to help them get started on the right track.

remain flexible

These three examples are designed to move people from a mindset of normal church expectations into a life of MissioRelate. Of course, not everyone will choose to take the journey, but you don't want lack of clarity to be the reason that people resist. (See Appendix E for some examples of various tools that you can use to help people along this journey.) You want the path to be clear and as concrete as possible, while at the same time leaving room for flexibility for the realities of life (those ups and downs that are naturally a part of any journey with Jesus in our fallen world).

Stubborn folks - For those who have no desire to move forward on the journey even after understanding it, they can remain a part of normal small groups or fulfill some form of service in the church. Whether they remain in the church or leave is usually something that takes care of itself. For smaller organic churches, it is usually best to help these people find a church that works for them. In most established churches, there is some role that they can play. Such people are typically middle adopters who don't like change. They need to see something new in action for a season before they are willing to participate. What might feel like resistance or even rebellion may actually be an expression of how a person is wired.

Tradition and context - To get that flywheel moving a little, church leaders must work together as a team to develop a process that fits their tradition, context and how much MissioRelate has become a part of the life of their church. When first starting out, the process will be much more programmatic, like the first two examples above. The churches of 3000 and 250 are primarily equipping people who come to the church through more traditional means. As the missional small groups become established, more people will participate in the life of the church in organic relational ways, leading to natural conversations with people in their neighborhoods and other life connections. This means that people will enter into the life of the church through these relationships and many will actually start their journey through the informal connections with a small group. When this happens, do not try to force those who join organically into the much more programmatic process. You will need to adapt some form of the third example above (the organic approach) for those who join your church through MissioRelate.

common elements to a path

Whatever path you develop, create something that works for you and avoid copying what others do by adopting their structure. I encourage churches to take the time to develop their own language. I always find it interesting when I visit a rural Midwestern church that has adopted the language and imagery that has been developed by a church in Southern California or by the denominational headquarters in Nashville. You will get much more buy-in if your people are a part of the process of developing the language.

At the same time, there are essential elements to moving people through the stories and into MissioRelate which are all shared by the three examples above. Most churches will either use books, materials and curriculum to help create experiences that move people into the life of MissioRelate (See Appendix E) but the path is not comprised of resources like this. The path is about having simple ways that everyone understands that aims at the life of MissioRelate. To identify these elements, let's return to the journey diagram, found on the next page.

Entering the airport

All three examples have very clear points of entry. In some cases, the entry points include formal church experiences, similar to a formal entry into an airport. In other cases, they are more organic and are based on relational connections, like the process of boarding a plane at a small regional or municipal airport. An established church might move people into MissioRelate in a linear fashion, assuming that people will almost always begin the journey through the ticketing area of the Sunday service. As missional groups are established, it will grow messy. People will enter into the life of the church in all kinds of

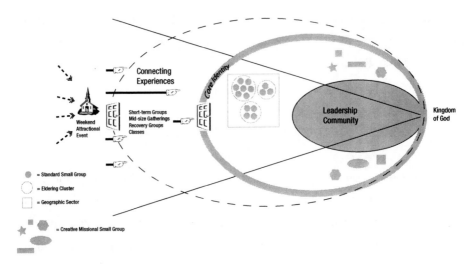

organic, unpredictable ways. This church will discover entry points in places they never knew they had before. In other words, any established church—no matter its size—might start out with formal processes of entering the life of MissioRelate (the ticketing counter, simple concourses and boarding area). But as they develop MissioRelate, relational processes for boarding planes will develop and entry into the life of the church will become less formal, similar to boarding a plane at a municipal airport. The formal processes might very well remain, but the new, less formal process will become commonplace.

However one enters the airport and boards the plane, it remains crucial to clearly communicate with everyone what they are doing and how best to enjoy the plane ride. Even when riding on a small propeller plane, everyone hears the basic safety instructions. Remember that clarity is key. (This is where the two doorways in the diagram above are essential to understand.)

Doorway #1: Vision introduction

Whether in a programmatic or an organic situation, there must be a first doorway for people to enter into the life of the church. In a programmatic situation, this doorway might be something like a membership or introduction to church life class. In an organic situation, it would be something informal between a house church leader and the person joining the group. The goal of this doorway is to introduce the journey and help people take initial steps.

At the first door, it is crucial to communicate what your church is about and the long term vision to equip people for life in missional small groups. You don't want to water down the vision. But at the same time, you want to validate the initial steps required to help people move into the MissioRelate vision. The emphasis of the first door is the communication of the core identity of the church and the desire to equip people in the basics of doing relationships in a healthy way.

Journey experiences

On the other side of this door are the connecting experiences. Again, these can be either formal and programmed or they can be organic and highly relational. A church might start out with a programmatic approach, but as they move along, they will find that organic relational connections occur within missional communities that help people move into a missional way of life.

The goal of these connecting experiences is to provide opportunities for people to become awakened to a new reality, to discover a different way of living. They might hear about the vision as they pass through the first door, but they won't actually grasp this new reality without a new experience.

Doorway #2: Core identity formation

At the second doorway, the goal is to help people discover the core identity of what you are becoming as a church. (Please note that I used the word "discover." I specifically did not say that people are *taught* the core identity of the church. Most churches don't need more disseminated information or Bible information explaining theologically nuances. Instead, what is needed is a shaping of our lives around the biblical story so that we can enter into an imagination of MissioRelate.) It's vital to your success to help people see themselves in that story so they can envision a MissioRelate church from and within their context. This cannot be prescribed to people by communicating loads of information. Instead, it must be caught as people discover together what their core identity is as God's missional people.

This door is far more than a membership class where people hear about the history and key beliefs of your denomination. While there may be a place for that, at this point people need to enter into a "reshaping process" so that they understand what it means to take the next steps toward mission. This is where a line is drawn in the sand and people see that moving ahead on mission is not the same as what is found across America. It involves counting the cost, discipleship, spiritual formation, and self-sacrifice. Is it popular Christianity? No, but people need to see what it really takes to live the life of MissioRelate up front or they will get into it and feel duped. Would you not take ten people who really want to do it than 100 people who just think that they do? The ten can serve as a seedbed creating a new way of being on mission (through the experiments of Chapter 10) for others to enter into at a later date.

Traditionally, a "line in the sand" process is called *catechesis*, but this is not the sort that you might find in any of the church traditions we've known. When the church first began the practice of catechism, it was for the purpose of reshaping a person's imagination around the biblical story. In many ways, today we need to have our imaginations shifted for mission. We must provide people with an opportunity to discover what it means to be missional, giving them the choice to reshape their lives around practices that will prepare their for lives for mission (Chapter 13).

At first, this Core Identify Formation will occur very informally. Last weekend, I was training leaders at a church in Virginia and the pastor was using my book *Missional Small Groups* for this purpose. He meets with leaders who are open to go beyond the normal group experience and walks through the four stories with them. Then, he helps their groups move through the reshaping process whereby they identify and develop missional practices. The key to getting the Core Identify Formation flywheel moving is having lots and lots of conversations with both leaders and their groups.

Eventually, the Core Identity Formation process will be more formalized. For example, I don't think it is too much to invite people into a 26-week core identity shaping process. The first 13 weeks would be class focused on hearing the grand missional story of the Scriptures, allowing people to process what it might mean to be "on mission" today. It would help people hear and retell the story of God's great missional love, how Jesus came to fulfill that mission, and how the Spirit carries out that mission today. The second 13-week segment would focus on helping people establish disciplines for mission (introduced in Chapter 13). This could be done in a classroom setting or in small groups.[1]

Core identity is not shaped quickly or even painlessly. Belief structures must be examined to see how we live our lives and look hard at the fact that our beliefs and the way we live are incongruent. Alan Roxburgh points out the need for cultivating a core identity in our churches quite well:

> In our day, cultivating an identity around a biblical narrative will need to be done within a framework like the one encountered by the people of God in Babylon. The single most significant element in that period of the Exile was the people's emerging capacity to reclaim their primary stories from a context of loss. The removal of the Jewish people from Jerusalem and its environs by Nebuchadnezzar along with the destruction of the Temple and the flattening the city's walls precipitated a crisis of massive proportions for Israel. The very meaning and nature of their beliefs and practices were called into question at fundamental levels.[2]

Our churches today, whether mired in traditional structures or venturing out in creative methods, are set in a special time. We are searching for what it means to be God's people in a context that no longer cares much about what we have to say as a church. We live in a time of exile and the core identity of the church is no longer clear. Our imaginations need an immersion in this reality so that we can see a new future for what God has for his people. The story of God has been lost—even in our churches—and we cannot simply throw people into groups, call them missional, and give them something to do. That will only replicate what we already have. We need to be reshaped (the point of Chapter 3).

Our missional future will arise as we rally around this core identity and new patterns of practicing our faith. It will lead to creative experiments of missional community. And it will lead to new forms of being the church.

closing thoughts

I could end this book with a nice story of a MissioRelate church or a summary that ties everything up in a neat package. But I'm not going to do that. I want to end the book right here on the theme surrounding the doorway of core identity for three reasons.

First, I want you to put this book down thinking about the concept of core identity and how you can immerse your people in an *experience* that prepares them for a missional future. Don't design a sermon series on it! Instead, think about the key leaders and innovators in your church who can lead the way with fresh experiments. Consider ten or fifteen people who need to be immersed in this imagination. How might this happen? Most leaders don't think this way and I want to challenge you to do so.

The second reason I have chosen to end this book on the theme of core identity is because I believe that this is the central theme of this book. As I wrote in the preface, this book was a bit of a writing accident. Likewise, the fact that I now see core identity as central to these chapters is not something I intended. The things we do to lead others shapes our core identity. As we put these alternative patterns into practice to turn the flywheel, we will create a new culture in our groups. But also we become different and we will not be left the same.

The third and final reason I end abruptly on this theme of core identity is that I don't want to give the impression that this story is complete. I fully believe that we are on a journey together and that there is much to learn about what God wants to do through us. More needs to be experienced and then written. My prayer is that this book is a conversation starter. Let's all allow the Spirit to reshape our core identity for life in MissioRelate and then let's share it with each other.

Practicing MissioRelate as Leaders

This appendix aims to point you toward a doable way of adopting the elements laid out in this book to create an environment that will facilitate MissioRelate. To get started, it is important to be realistic. Most churches will not be able to implement all ten of the elements of the MissioRelate found in part 2 of this book at once. In fact, I doubt any will. Instead, I encourage you to process these elements with a team of three to five leaders in order to identify three that should be a priority over the next year. Then, on an annual basis, assess how well you are pushing the flywheel and determine what needs to be done next.

To help you assess and make plans for implementing a process that fits your church, I have included some things that I have seen other churches do as they worked through earlier editions of this material. Each of the ten elements includes a confession of a value related to that element in the process; a few practical steps that are being implemented; and a priority ranking on a scale of 1 to 100. Write your own value statement, identify a few practical steps to consider and rank its priority. Here are some examples:

MissioRelate Value: Asking Missional Questions (Chapter 5)
Because we value people, we will practice rhythms of relationality that prioritize people over programs. This means that:

- Pastoral staff members who work with groups will begin to ask different questions about what is going on in their groups. They will spend the time to develop relationships with a few group leaders to really understand what is happening in groups.

— Priority Rating: 80

MissioRelate Value: Christ's Presence (Chapter 6)

Because we value the presence of Christ, the kinds of groups that we will emphasize are those that seek his presence. This means that groups will:

- Gather regularly to meet in the presence of Christ. We will encourage groups to meet weekly. Twice per month groups would be identified as social groups that have a different status.
- Establish groups through a team-based leadership approach grounded on the scripture, "where 2 or 3 gather in my name there I am also."[1]

— Priority Rating: 65

MissioRelate Value: Discipleship (Chapter 7)

Because we value discipleship, wholeness and growth of individuals and communities, we will promote environments that help people simplify their lives in the midst of a culture of complexity:

- We will organize pastoral oversight geographically.
- Coaches will work with groups who are in close proximity.
- We will encourage groups to gather around proximity and share life together outside the meetings. Exceptions to this rule are groups of people whose life-stage allows them extra time than the average person in our culture.

— Priority Rating: 55

MissioRelate Value: Dealing with People's Real Lives (Chapter 8)

Because we want to lead people from where they are into a new vision, we will give them steps that they can take and not just talk about radical visions and goals. Therefore:

- We will refuse to grow bigger just for the sake of growing bigger. We will not start groups just to start groups.
- We will cast a radical vision of being on mission with God in this world, talking about the scriptural call for social justice, racial and socioeconomic reconciliation, community transformation, and being present in our neighborhoods.
- We will assess where people are and set up practical steps that they can take that will move them into the vision of mission.

— Priority Rating: 85

MissioRelate Value: Space to Answer Life Questions: (Chapter 9)
Because we value self-discovery, we will:

- We refuse to prescribe top-down methods for groups that are interested in going beyond normal small group life.
- We will walk with these groups so they are clear on what the goal is and they can understand the boundaries and not get off track.

— Priority Rating: 75

MissioRelate Value: Experiments (Chapter 10)
Because we know that the Spirit is alive in our people, we will identify those who are gifted and called to experiment with alternative forms of group life and then empower them to do so. Therefore, we will:

- Equip people in the discovery and use of their gifts.
- Meet with these people and identify various experiments that we can try out.
- Help their groups listen to the creativity of the Spirit as they engage

their world with the Gospel and allow for creative group patterns to arise.

— Priority Rating: 50

MissioRelate Value: Relational Intelligence (Chapter 11)

Because we value healthy connections, we will invite people to learn how to do relationships well. We will do this by:

- Holding two 40-day small group campaigns per year to help disconnected people experiment with community and discover what it means to love a few other people.
- Creating mid-size environments that make it safe for people to move from one space to another.
- Train people in what it means to love one another so that they have the skills to actually do community in healthy ways.

— Priority Rating: 40

MissioRelate Value: Relational Eldering (Chapter 12)

Because we value the people we lead, we will lead relationally, investing in the whole person, never leaving a leader without relational support. We will do this through pastors and coaches who:

- Develop Elders who live in such a way that they can invest in the communities and support other leaders.
- Work with Elders to discover the patterns of missional community that best fit the local context.

— Priority Rating: 70

MissioRelate Value: Spiritual Formation of Individuals (Chapter 13)
Because we value equipping of individuals, we will develop rhythms that promote life as resident aliens whose primary citizenship is the kingdom of God not the American culture. Therefore we will:

- Consistently teach people about the core foundations of the faith and the implications these have on the church's priorities and structure.
- Offer Freedom Encounters that will help people move beyond past hurts.
- Develop a way to equip people in healthy relationship patterns, whether through a class or with small group curriculum.

— Priority Rating: 90

MissioRelate Value: Seeking God (Chapter 14)
Because we value the God who wages war against evil, we will fight with God by developing environments where people can seek God's face through worship and prayer:

- We will train our groups in practical ways to worship in small groups.
- We will hold quarterly times of prayer and worship for 3-5 groups to come together and seek God.

— Priority Rating: 65

You could do something very similar to the above example. For each of the chapters in Part 2 of the book, identify what you could do to actually implement the point of view presented there. Then rate them on a scale of one to ten. Identify those that are most important to your next steps as a leadership group and then focus on one or two over the next six months.

Going Deeper with Additional Resources

There are lots of good books on small groups you can read, but this list is different. It includes books that you may not have immediately thought would help you develop missional group life. I've only listed two or three for each of the chapters in Part 2. If you implement the team processing strategy outlined in Appendix A, you might find it helpful to use some of these books to go deeper.

For Small Group Leaders
- *Missional Small Groups: Becoming a Community that Makes a Difference in the World* by M. Scott Boren
- *Missional Small Groups Study Guide* by M. Scott Boren
- *Leading Missional Small Groups: Developing the Skills to Lead a Group that Make a Difference in the World* by M. Scott Boren (Forthcoming 2013)

Chapter 5: Asking Different Questions
- *Introducing the Missional Church* by Alan Roxburgh and M. Scott Boren
- *A Hidden Wholeness: The Journey Toward an Undivided Life* by Parker J. Palmer

Chapter 6: Gather Around the Presence
- *The Pocket Guide to Burnout-free Small Group Leadership: How To Gather a Core Team and Lead from the Second Chair* by Michael Mack
- *Present Perfect: Finding God in the Now* by Gregory A. Boyd

Chapter 7: Focus on Discipleship
- *Sacred Companions: The Gift of Spiritual Friendship and Direction* by David Benner
- *Organic Disciplemaking: Mentoring Others into Spiritual Maturity and Leadership* by Dennis McCallum and Jessica Lowery

- *John Wesley's Class Meeting: A Model for Making Disciples* by D. Michael Henderson
- *Cultivating a Life for God: Multiplying Disciples through Life Transformation Groups* by Neil Cole

Chapter 8: Deal with Reality
- *Foolishness to the Greeks: The Gospel and Western Culture* by Lesslie Newbigin
- *The Gospel in a Pluralist Society* by Lesslie Newbigin
- *Habits of the Heart: Individualism and Commitment in American Life* by Robert Bellah, et. al.
- *The Saturated Self: Dilemmas of Identity in Contemporary Life* by Kenneth Gergen
- *Inter-Personal Divide: The Search for Community in a Technological Age* by Michael Bugeja
- *Bowling Alone: The Collapse and Revival of American Community* by Robert Putnam
- *Community: Seeking Safety in an Insecure World* by Zygmunt Bauman

Chapter 9: Help People Answer Their Questions
- *Community: The Structure of Belonging* by Peter Block
- *The Search to Belong: Rethinking Intimacy, Community, and Small Groups* by Joseph Myers
- *Becoming Community: Biblical Meditations and Applications in Modern Life* by Karl A. Schultz

Chapter 10: Encourage Experiments
- *Missional: Joining God in the Neighborhood* by Alan Roxburgh
- *Launching Missional Communities: A Field Guide* by Mike Breen and Alex Absalom

Chapter 11: Equip People in Relational Intelligence

- *Making Room for Life* by Randy Frazee
- *Caring Enough to Confront*: *How To Understand and Express Your Deepest Feelings Toward Others* by David Augsburger
- *Relationships*: *A Mess Worth Making* by Tim Lane and Paul Tripp
- *Nonviolent Communication*: *A Language of Life* by Marshall B. Rosenberg
- *The DNA of Relationships* by Gary Smalley
- *Becoming Human* by Jean Vanier

Chapter 12: Empower Elders

- *Missional Map Making*: *Skills for Leading in Times of Transition* by Alan Roxburgh
- *The Leadership Ellipse* by Robert Fryling

Chapter 13: Practice Mission

- *After You Believe*: *Why Christian Character Matters* by N. T. Wright
- *Practicing Our Faith*: *A Way of Life for a Searching People* edited by Dorothy Bass
- *Spiritual Formation as if the Church Mattered*: *Growing in Christ through Community* by James C. Wilhoit
- *Sacred Rhythms*: *Arranging Our Lives for Spiritual Transformation* by Ruth Haley Barton

Chapter 14: Embrace Mystery

- *Christ Plays in Ten Thousand Places* by Eugene Peterson
- *SoulTalk*: *The Language God Longs for Us To Speak* by Larry Crabb

Going Deeper with The Relational Way

In my book, *The Relational Way*, I introduce the following structural myths and contrast them with relational truths. When church leaders focus their energy on the structural myths, the groups that result are what I call normal. But when church leaders develop the relational truths, their groups will begin to live out a new kind of mission in relationship, or what I call in this book MissioRelate.

Structural Myth #1: Doing the right thing (a small group program) without consideration of the right way (the relational way) will produce community.

The Relational Truth: God's relational kingdom is a product of leaders who establish a way of living that stands in contrast to the culture.

If we genuinely want to move beyond the normal to produce missional group life, then we all must realize that we have learned to play church rhythms that don't actually produce this kind of life. Those of us steeped in the life of the church know only how to start and run programs. If this mentality prevails as we develop and lead small groups, then our results will be less than satisfying.

Structural Myth #2: Groups will succeed if they are built around a specific practical strategy or method.

The Relational Truth: Relational kingdom groups are based upon the reality of Christ's presence within those groups.

I have seen all kinds of strategies and curriculum promising groups that result in dynamic life. But the kind of life that I hope to see is founded upon the reality that Christ shows up in a group and the people in the group know how to respond together to his presence. This moves us beyond questions about DVD curriculum, the use of the web for groups or other creative ways to get groups going. The question is not about methods but about presence. If we get his presence right, then lots of different methods can be used.

Structural Myth #3: Meeting in small groups is the central source of biblical community.

The Relational Truth: Relational kingdom life requires the church to address how people do life, not just how they do small groups.

So much of our current focus on small group strategies surrounds on how to set up and lead small group meetings. And while good group meetings are better than nothing, there must be more to church than good meetings. Our job as leaders is to help people live in mission, not just help them get involved in our meetings.

Structural Myth #4: Building a new small group ministry structure on top of old stories of church will transform a church and build community.

The Relational Truth: Relational kingdom life through small groups is founded upon a missional base which compels a church to write a new story of being the people of God.

I have found this truth to be one of the most difficult for church leaders to fully grasp. We have a tendency to see small group strategies as a technical change, whereby we develop a small group strategy in addition to what the church is already doing. We fail to see the need for adaptive or deep change that requires us to rethink how church and church leadership operates. For every church, the challenge to implement this truth will be unique. Each church has its own heritage and specific history with which to contend. However, there are some basic ways to learn to lead according to this truth and discover how to write this new kind of story.

Structural Myth #5: Small group community is best fostered in a context whereby the group members focus solely on ministering to the needs of one another.

The Relational Truth: Relational kingdom groups follow Jesus' mission to the world and develop deep, contagious fellowship.

God's life is an overflowing community. He gave freely of himself so that we might have life. If we are truly experiencing God's life in our midst, he will move us to give that life to others who do not have it. Small groups that only focus on experiencing community within a limited group of people may very well find God there, but they are missing out on how God is moving in this world to transform people and all of creation. Church leaders must set up groups systems that facilitate this truth or our selfish tendencies will cause groups to turn in on themselves to protect and maintain their current experience.

Structural Myth #6: Small groups can develop biblical community without an overt dependence upon the Holy Spirit.

The Relational Truth: Relational kingdom groups are a product of the dynamic life of the Holy Spirit.

This truth can be clarified by a simple question: Do we believe that God is alive today in our midst or do we see God as an eternal truth that we are to talk about? To move beyond the normal group experience, we need a concentrated focus on the reality that God is alive today and doing a work in the midst of normal people of our churches. As leaders, our job is not to make that happen, but to facilitate conversations so that people realize what the Spirit is doing.

Structural Myth #7: The small group/large group structure is all that is needed to develop community in a church.

The Relational Truth: God's relational kingdom connects people on four levels.

Much has been written about the pattern of connecting people in large group worship and small group community. However, if we shape our churches to connect people in structures alone, we miss the relational dynamics of how God made us. We must equip people to connect on four levels: publicly, socially, personally, and intimately. Some have emphasized personal and intimate connections in small groups without recognizing the importance of helping people get connected socially. Without healthy social connections, relationships will feel forced and unnatural. And if there is anything that cannot be forced, it's relationships.

Structural Myth #8: Small group leaders will flourish when they are managed properly by coaches and pastors.

The Relational Truth: In God's relational kingdom, small group leaders need someone who invests in them to empower them for mission.

This truth is founded upon the need to invest in leaders within groups. Leaders that lead in isolation lead normal groups and experience normal life. Leaders that are being mentored, challenged, and equipped have the ability to invest in others, develop teams, and discover what God is doing . . . and move into new ways of being God's people. Church leaders must establish a rhythm of mentoring from the top down so that this life flows into the groups. This is not so much about setting up a coaching structure, but about establishing a way of investing in people, much like the Apostle Paul did when he established elders in a local church.

———————————

Structural Myth #9: Equipping that solely addresses 'right Christian thinking' will adequately prepare people for relational kingdom living and fruitful small group life.

The Relational Truth: In God's relational kingdom, equipping the people means we must prepare them to walk as aliens and strangers in this world.

Church leaders know how to help people think correctly. We even know how to help people behave ethically. But the kind of equipping for mission in relationships requires us to equip people to walk according to a pattern that is not shaped by this world. We must learn to create environments where people learn how the way they do life works against God's mission so that they can relearn how to live so that they can get in line with God's mission.

———————————

Structural Myth #10: Small groups will grow and multiply if they serve as a place to discuss the Bible and connect people in relationships.

The Relational Truth: In God's relational kingdom, groups and individuals are mobilized into units for spiritual warfare.

To live on mission in this world is to stand against the powers and principalities of this world. Groups that live in community and act as conduits of God's love are establishing kingdom of God life in the midst of the kingdom of death. Groups must be empowered, equipped, and supported for this spiritual warfare.

Community Practices

The following is a brief summary for the various practices introduced in chapters 7-9 of *Missional Small Groups*.

rhythms of missional communion

Worship
The church knows how to do formal worship. But what about worship in a living room? What about worship with friends?

Practicing the Presence
Nothing sets God's people apart like the presence of God. But do we actually expect to meet with God in our groups? If not, why not? What might it look like to meet with God regularly and go beyond the Bible study mentality?

Alone Together
How do we practice silence and solitude as a private discipline but do it together? Usually we think of this individualistically, but there is a way of being "alone together" before God. How do we practice this?

Listening Together
How does a group of people practice the art of listening to God? How might God speak to "you" for "me?" And how do we create space for such an experience?

Simplicity
The way we spend our time and money relates directly to our worship of God. In our culture we idolize things. If we don't let others in on this part of our lives, we won't every change this pattern.

Jesus' Meal

Traditions usually address this in one of five ways in their formal services. There is an alternative way of doing this around a meal, while at the same time not throwing out any of the current formal traditions of communion.

Sabbath

Our ability to rest relates to our ability to trust both God and others. This practice seems to have shaped the Old Testament people of God as much as any other. What bearing does this have on us as a New Testament people? How can we practice Sabbath today in our 24/7 world?

rhythms of missional relating

A Primary Group

Most people have lots of shallow relationships, but they lack a primary group of people who will walk with them and point them toward the kingdom.

A Safe Place

How do we create relationships that are safe, where there is both honesty and freedom along with accountability and challenge?

Saying Hello

Greeting one another well is about developing listening skills. Often this simple piece is overlooked by church leadership and it undermines people's ability to relate to one another.

Pressing through Conflict

Relationships are messy. Of this there is no doubt. We must learn to work through conflict and refuse to give up on others. This requires some new relationship skills.

Face-to-Face contact

Community in our culture must call for face-to-face contact. At the same time we must deal with the reality of how the internet and cell phones are impacting our ability to interact with one another.

Build Up Each Other

Encouragement that flows out of the heart of God through his people for others is essential to God's kind of community. What does this look like in practical terms?

Family Life and Small Groups

Too many times, the group is seen as separate from the family connected to each group member. If true relationships are going to be developed then the group must determine how to connect the two.

Initiation into the Community

How does a group practice baptism in a way that communicates that new Christians are being initiated into Christ *and* into Christ's community?

rhythms of missional engagement

Moving into the Neighborhood

One of the keys to engagement is just being present in our neighborhoods. This requires the risk of just putting ourselves out there and engage others.

Focus

We need to learn to say "no" to a lot of "good" stuff in order to be involved in God's mission. This may mean saying "no" to some "church" activities so that we have time to engage the people and needs in our world.

Speaking Peace

We are present in the neighborhood as agents of peace in the midst of turmoil. What does this look like? What are some ways that work in our specific contexts to take peace to people?

Observe

What is God already doing in and through the people and systems around you? We don't have to generate God's mission. God is already at work. We only need to see what the Spirit is doing and get involved.

Hospitality

Opening up our homes to one another is essential to knowing each other. How do we do this in our time-starved world? How do we eat together in our fast-food world? We must address the reality of these questions.

Righting Wrongs

Ask the question: What does God want to do? There are injustices in our world that are crying out for God's people to show up and offer justice.

Speaking the Gospel

Instead of a canned approach, we must learn to communicate Christ in relationships with others, viewing them as equals, not as people to be won over to our way.

Curriculum, Tools, and Resources to Support MissioRelate

I have already developed some tools to help people move through the process introduced in Chapter 18 and I will be developing more.

Visit www.mscottboren.com to find these tools, and those by others that I find especially helpful in moving people toward this vision.

Introduction

1. This stage was explored in my next book called *The Relational Way*.
2. On this note, it is crucial to notice that the wisest leaders of the organic church movement admit this fact. But the reality is that most who take this option don't realize this until it is too late. By that time they have alienated the traditional church that formed them and then they find themselves a part of something that is just as fallible and sometimes even more problematic.

Chapter One

1. Jim Collins, *Good to Great: Why Some Companies Make the Leap ... and Others Don't* (New York: Harper Business, 2001), p. 164-165.
2. Collins, p. 169.
3. Collins, p. 178.
4. Parker Palmer, *A Hidden Wholeness* (San Francisco: Jossey-Bass, 2006), p. 74-75.

Chapter Two

1. M. Scott Boren, *Missional Small Groups* (Grand Rapids: Baker Books, 2010). p. 39.
2. Boren, p. 40
3. Boren, p. 41
4. Boren, p. 43

Chapter Four

1. Resources by Steve Sjogren are especially helpful when looking to create such outreach support.
2. See the excellent tool by Mike Breen and Alex Absalom, *Launching Missional Communities: A Field Guide* (Pawley's Island: 3DM Publishing, 2011).

Chapter Five

1. This is another way of envisioning the "flywheel effect."
2. Peter Block, *Community* (San Francisco: Berrett-Koehler, 2009), p. 29.
3. Block, p. 11.
4. These 21 practices are found in chapters 7-9 in *Missional Small Groups* (Grand Rapids: Baker Books, 2010).
5. You might think my use of the word "missional" in these rhythmic labels is repetitive. I have used the word to confront an inaccurate mindset. Many assume that being missional is reaching out to people outside one's own socioeconomic or people group. When we use "missional" in this way, we might as well use the word "evangelism" or "outreach." An imagination that is shaped by a biblical view of God's mission is much more than that.

Chapter Six

1. See my earlier book *How do We Get There From Here* (pages 49-66) for detailed analysis of these various models.
2. *The Relational Way* (Houston: TOUCH Publications, 1998), p. 62-63.
3. Michael Mack, *The Pocket Guide to Burnout-Free Small Group Leadership* (Houston: TOUCH Publications, 2009), p. 35-37.

Chapter Seven

1. Elizabeth O'Connor, *Call to Commitment* (San Francisco, CA: Harper & Row, 1985), p. 34.
2. O'Connor, p. 128
3. O'Connor, p. 128
4. Dennis McCallum and Jessica Lowery, *Organic Disciplemaking* (Houston, TX: Touch Publications, 2006), p. 19-20.
5. Jimmy Seibert, *The Church Can Change the World* (Waco, TX: Antioch Community Church, 2008), p. 164.
6. Neil Cole, *Search and Rescue* (Grand Rapids, MI: Baker Books, 2008).
7. John Westley, *John Wesley's Class Meeting* (Napanee, IN: Francis Asbury Press, 1997).
8. Greg Ogden, *Discipleship Essentials* (Downers Grove, IL: IVP Books, 2007).

Chapter Eight

1. Ted Haggard, *Dog Training, Fly Fishing and Sharing Christ in the 21st Century* (Nashville, TN: Thomas Nelson, 2008).

Chapter Nine

1. Matthew 28:18-20
2. Luke 10:27
3. Luke 10:28
4. Matthew 28:19a
5. Matthew 28:19b

Chapter Ten

1. These categories of change are adapted from Everett M. Rogers, *Diffusion of Innovations*, 4th ed. (New York: Free Press, 1995).
2. Ibid.
3. For more on this, read Chapters 14 and 15 of *Introducing the Missional Church* by Alan Roxburgh and myself.
4. This material is quoted from the seminar notes by Alan Roxburgh entitled *Mission-Shaped Groups: Structures for Mission-Shaped Formation* with light editing. Used with permission.

Chapter Eleven

1. Gary Smalley, *The DNA of Relationships* (Wheaton: Tyndale, 2004), p. 10.

2. Will Miller and Glen Sparks, *Refrigerator Rights* (South Barrington: Willow Creek Association, 2008).
3. Jonathan Wilson-Hartgrove, *The Wisdom of Stability* (Brewster: Paraclete Press, 2010).
4. Henri Nouwen, *Spiritual Formation* (San Francisco: HarperOne, 2010), p. 79.
5. There are lots of great materials that can help groups with this, but as I stated above, most of it comes from the world of marriage counseling. A great place to start is with Gary Smalley's book, *The DNA of Relationships*. At least there they try to apply these things to the realm of friendships.
6. This kind of training is especially important for people who are seeking to shift from Lifestyle Adjustment story to the Relational Revision story. In my book, *Missional Small Groups*, I provide practices that a group can begin. Those under the rhythm of that I call Missional Relating help a group do life differently so that they can learn to grow in love with one another.
7. Chapter 8 of *Missional Small Groups* is designed to get groups started on this path. If you want to deeper, the recent work of Alan Roxburgh in his book *Missional: Joining God in the Neighborhood* is helpful. He also has a companion workbook and a 13-week study on practicing hospitality.

Chapter Twelve
1. See *How Do We Get There from Here*, chapters 6.4 and 7.2 and *The Relational Way*, chapter 8.
2. Dr. Jim Egli, *Small Groups Big Impact* (Church Smart, 2011).
3. I find that the coaching resources by Tony Stoltzfus to be especially helpful on this topic, especially *Leadership Coaching* (Booksurge Publishing, 2005) and *Coaching Questions* (Pegasus Creative Arts, 2008).
4. Robert Fryling, *The Leadership Ellipse* (Downers Grove: IVP Books, 2010), p. 18.
5. Darrel Guder, editor, *Missional Church: A Vision for the Sending of the Church in North America* (Grand Rapids: Eerdmans, 1996). Specifically, this concept was derived from Chapter 7: *Missional Leadership*.

Chapter Thirteen
1. The benefits of this approach are numerous. First, it is the only way to come close to understanding where the people are so that we can meet them there and lead them into the revolution. Second, multiple voices are needed to generate a revolution. If there is only one voice, then people tend to rally around that person instead of embracing the message. Third, we have the benefit of multiple gifts and perspectives that are learning to work together. Fourth, those on this team are forced to lead by listening to one another, which is a pattern of life that should infiltrate the entire system of the church. This has impact upon the "senior pastor" model of church leadership. Having the "get-r-done" kind of leader who makes things happen can actually work against the kind of movement toward revolution that is deliberate. Yes such a leader might get things done, but people will only line up with the program and fail to embrace the way of revolution. People will rally around the individual leader rather than God.

2. Large venues only help people mentally grasp the vision for revolution. They don't equip them in the life patterns that line up with the revolution. For the larger crowd, identify four or five central points to the revolution and bang those points like big drums.

3. The idea is to boil down some of the crucial aspects of the vision outlined in a full-length book into bite sized chunks so that the stocker at Wal-Mart or the overworked executive can understand and embrace the vision.

4. N. T. Wright, *After You Believe* (San Francisco: HarperOne, 2010), p. 19-20.

5. Wright, 20.

6. In my book *Missional Small Groups*, I wrote about three basic rhythms that we need to develop with others and I identified seven specific practices or disciplines for each of these three rhythms. A list of the 21 community practices that I identify in Missional Small Groups are provided on the next three pages. In the corresponding study guide, groups will learn to develop these practices by starting with three and then building on that foundation.

Chapter Sixteen

1. While nesting isn't horrible, it most often it leads to complacency or a mindset to simply support whatever desires the people of the congregation might have.

Chapter Eighteen

1. *Missional Small Groups: A Study Guide for Making a Difference in the World.* Visit mscottboren.com or more information.

2. Alan Roxburgh, *Missional Map Making* (San Francisco: Jossey-Bass, 2010), p. 141.

Appendix A

1. See *The Pocket Guide to Burn-Out Free Small Group Leadership* by Michael Mack.

CPSIA information can be obtained at www.ICGtesting.com
Printed in the USA
LVOW131410090812

293678LV00007B/39/P